MINIMUM **DESIGN**

Series directed by
Andrea Branzi

Achille and Pier Giacomo CASTIGLIONI

Matteo Vercelloni

24 ORE Cultura

Cover
Mezzadro, Zanotta, 1971
Courtesy of Zanotta,
Nova Milanese

Published by
24 ORE Cultura srl

Editorial Director
Natalina Costa

Project Editor
Chiara Savino

Project Manager
Chiara Giudice
Anna Mainoli

Director of Production
Maurizio Bartomioli

Graphic design
Irma Robbiati

Page layout
Gianluca Turturo

Picture research and editing
Silvia Russo

Photolithography
Valter Montani

Editorial Assistant
Giorgia Montagna

English translation
by Sergio Knipe for Scriptum, Rome

© 2011 24 ORE Cultura srl, Pero (Milan), Italy

All rights reserved. No part of this book
may be reproduced in any form.

First edition: October 2011

ISBN 978-88-6648-025-9

Printed in Italy

MINIMUM DESIGN

Titles in the series
Franco Albini
Ron Arad
Achille and Pier Giacomo Castiglioni
Joe Colombo
Tom Dixon
Gio Ponti
Ettore Sottsass

Forthcoming titles
Alvar Aalto
Gae Aulenti
Andrea Branzi
Antonio Citterio
Michele De Lucchi
Stefano Giovannoni
Konstantin Grcic
Vico Magistretti
Angelo Mangiarotti
Enzo Mari
Alessandro Mendini
Carlo Mollino
Jasper Morrison
Eero Saarinen
Philippe Starck
Marco Zanuso

CONTENTS

4 | The Castiglioni Brothers
Andrea Branzi

22 | The Castiglioni Method

36 | Catalogue of Objects

38 | The Objects

118 | Selected References

The Castiglioni Brothers
Andrea Branzi

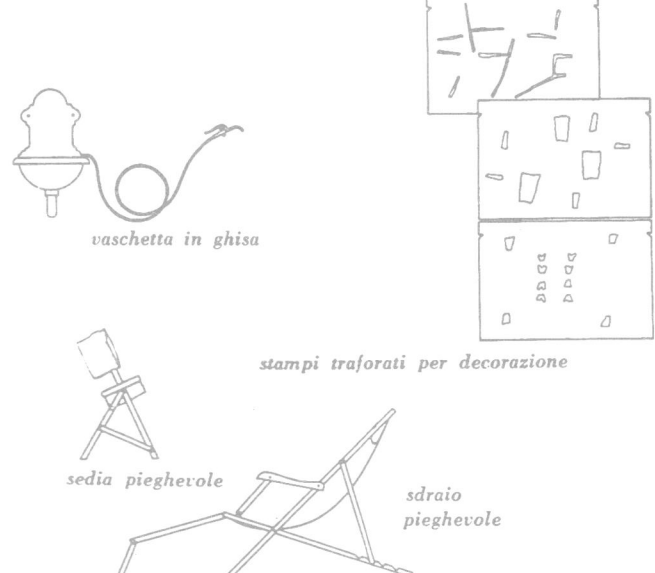

It is far from easy to interpret the work of the brothers Achille, Pier Giacomo and Livio Castiglioni, because behind their apparent ease as *bricoleurs* there lies a cultured and problematical form of design. This combines improvisation with a careful strategic approach that is parsimonious with stylistic hallmarks, which might be linked to a sort of *sarcastic rationalism.* It combines the subtle irony of reason with moments of powerful and almost Dada-like inspiration; and it combines modern radicalism with distinctly Milanese common sense—a keenness to discover the essential in things, as well as their satirical power. When observing things, the Castiglioni brothers seemed to discover both their *sense* and their *non-sense*. Without ever repeating the same design or motif, they made their objects easily recognizable, since they all share a capacity to convey a surplus of energy and ironic surprise. The Castiglioni studio in Piazza Castello, now the Achille Castiglioni Studio Museum, features a collection of tools, found objects and small masterpieces of anonymous design: hammers, scissors, agricultural implements and workwear items. This collection provided one of the starting points for the brothers' work of design. The latter was based on their willingness to set off from existing types of objects and tested mechanisms, as well as on their ability to situate these objects in an emptiness of meaning from which they could draw new life: a fishing rod, a bicycle saddle and the seat of a tractor could all be turned into *something different*—into new objects for a new mode of living.
One should not be misled by this apparently surrealist attitude, because in their work as designers the brothers actually valued tested experience, although they transcended it by freeing it through conjuring tricks and reviving it through a different functional dimension. The Castiglioni brothers not only knew how to turn readymades into objects of design, but also how to achieve the opposite: how to turn objects of design into readymades—completely new objects into found objects of sorts.
The Castiglioni brothers treated technology not as a myth but as a *naked king* that has nothing to do with hi-tech. Their technology could be displayed without the risk of it invading the fragile human environment, since it was harmless and amusing and conveyed common sense and surprise.
This was the real *sarcastic Italian rationalism*, which lacked a common methodology and language. Designers such as the Castiglioni brothers sought to teach industry the modesty of craftsmanship—without any of the rhetoric of large companies or of handicrafts—in order to almost naively extract essential mechanisms, as if they were simple pieces of good advice casually found in the (very wise) mind of the designer. In Italy this *rationalism* has always been synonymous with *simplicity* rather than scientific rigour.

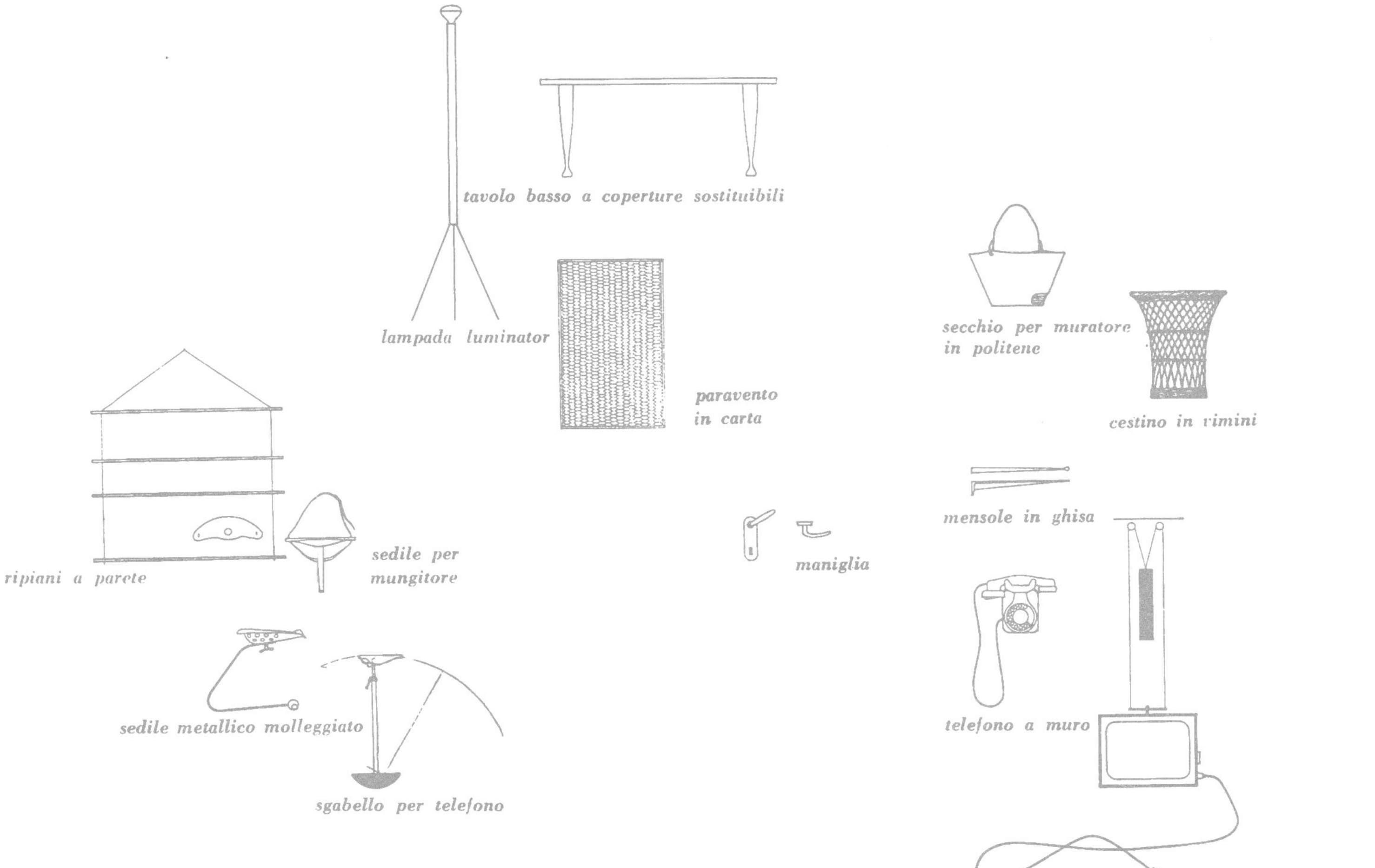

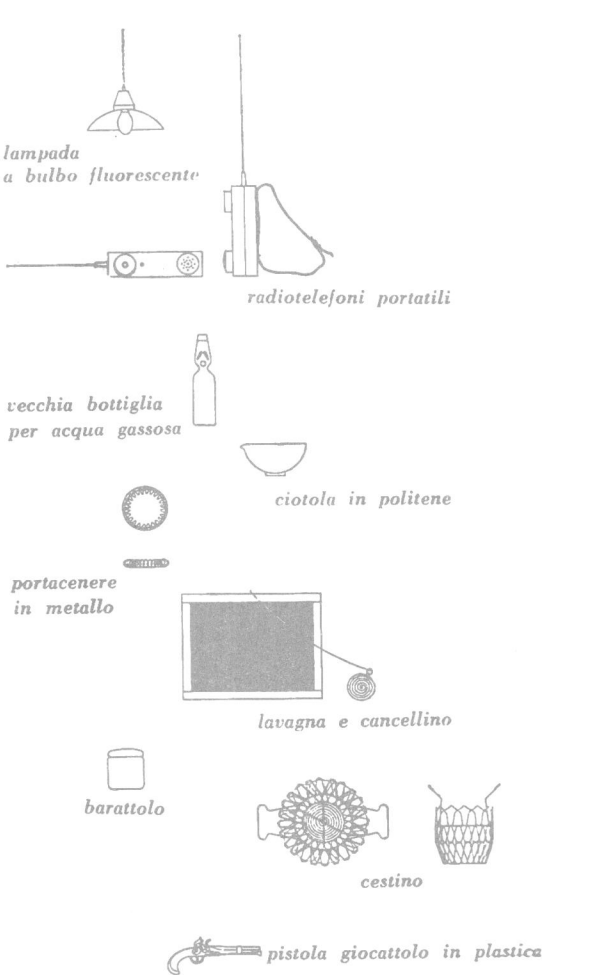

Like the Futurists, the Castiglioni brothers seemed to be saying "let us have fun: let us reinvent life's tools, because life and its tools have grown stupid and boring…" They were like those comedians who never laugh and accept the comical disasters and paradoxes of reality with a sense of the tragic.

Indeed, much talk has been made of the proximity of the work of the brothers to the heritage of Milanese Futurism. Both were shocking and taunting; both, I believe, harboured a secret pessimism towards modernity, which they deemed capable of constructing not any systems of certainty or new cathedrals, but only a dynamic scenario, the anarchical carnival of a *city that rises* endlessly and aimlessly—fuelled by a sort of trade in dead souls, as in Gogol's novel. If we put all the objects created by Achille and his brothers together, what emerges is not a cathedral but a horizontal landscape, a carousel which seems to stem from a secular and disenchanted view of man's fate; a verdict that is not necessarily pessimistic, but is rather reminiscent of the final ring a ring o' roses in Fellini's *8½,* which makes no sense and is all the more serene for this reason.

17

> If you're not curious, give up.
> If you're not interested in other people,
> in what they do and how they act,
> then the designer's life is not for you.
> Don't think you will become the inverters
> of the world. It isn't and should not be so.
> Start getting used to self-irony and self-criticism.
> […]
> Good projects spring not from the ambition
> to leave one's mark, but from the will
> to establish an exchange, even a small exchange,
> with the unknown person who will be using
> the object you have designed.
> Rest assured that research is everything
> and that each individual object produced
> is simply a stage and temporary stop rather
> than an ending. Forget about the idea of the
> artist's splendid isolation. Objects of design
> are the fruit of the joint efforts of many
> people with different expertises (technical,
> industrial, commercial and aesthetic).
> The work of the designer is the expressive
> synthesis of this collective work.

(*Come si diventa un bravo designer?* Achille Castiglioni)

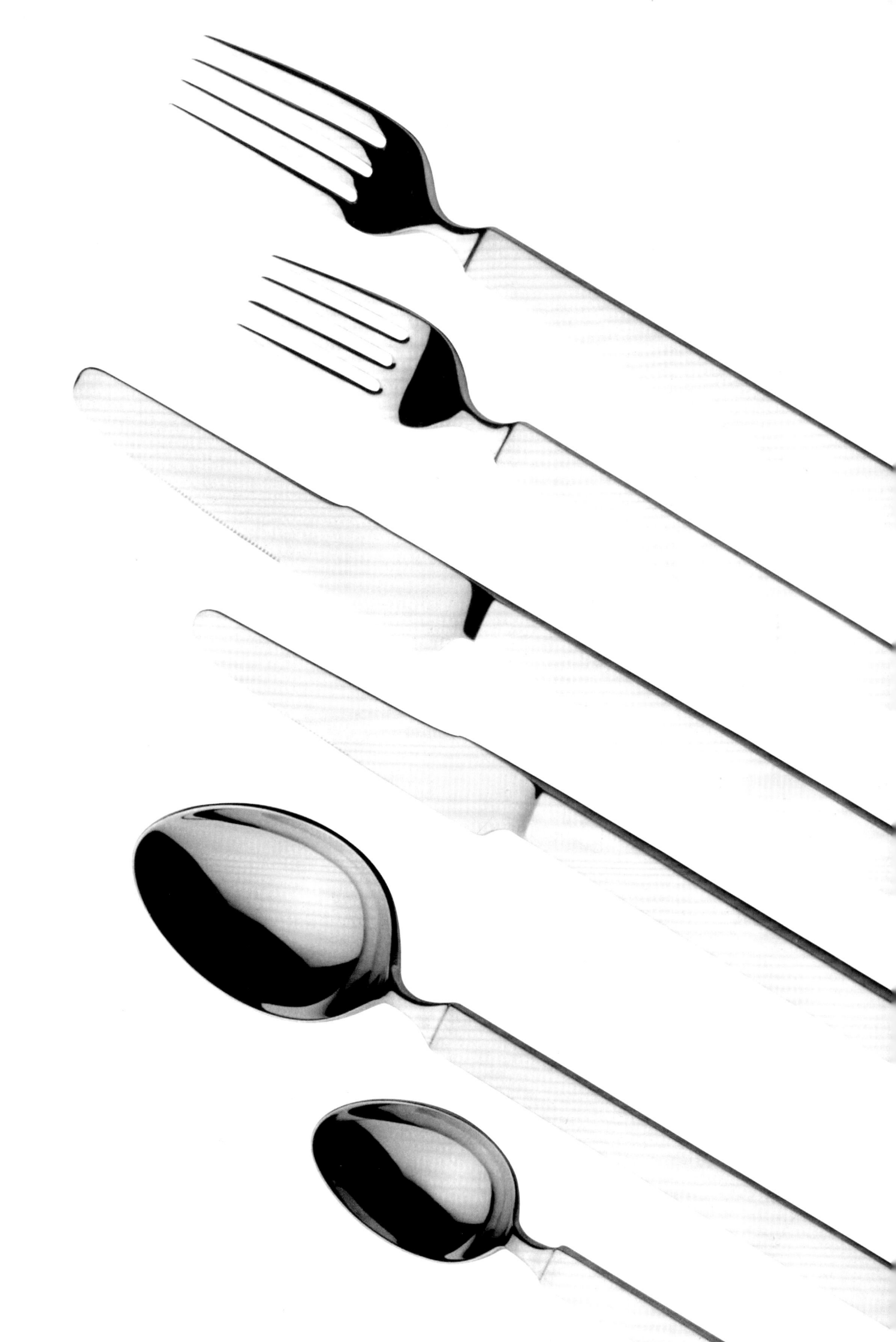

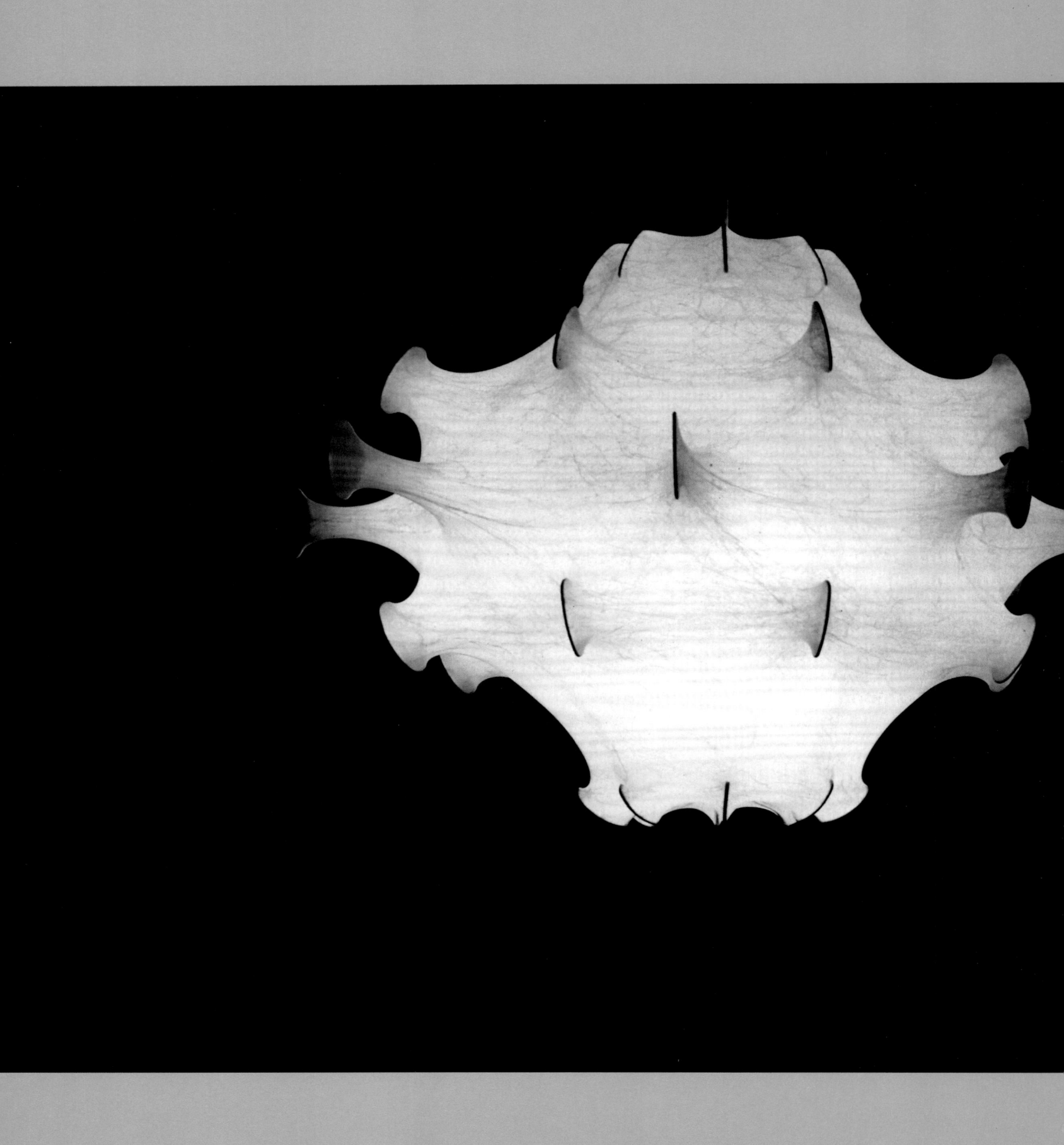

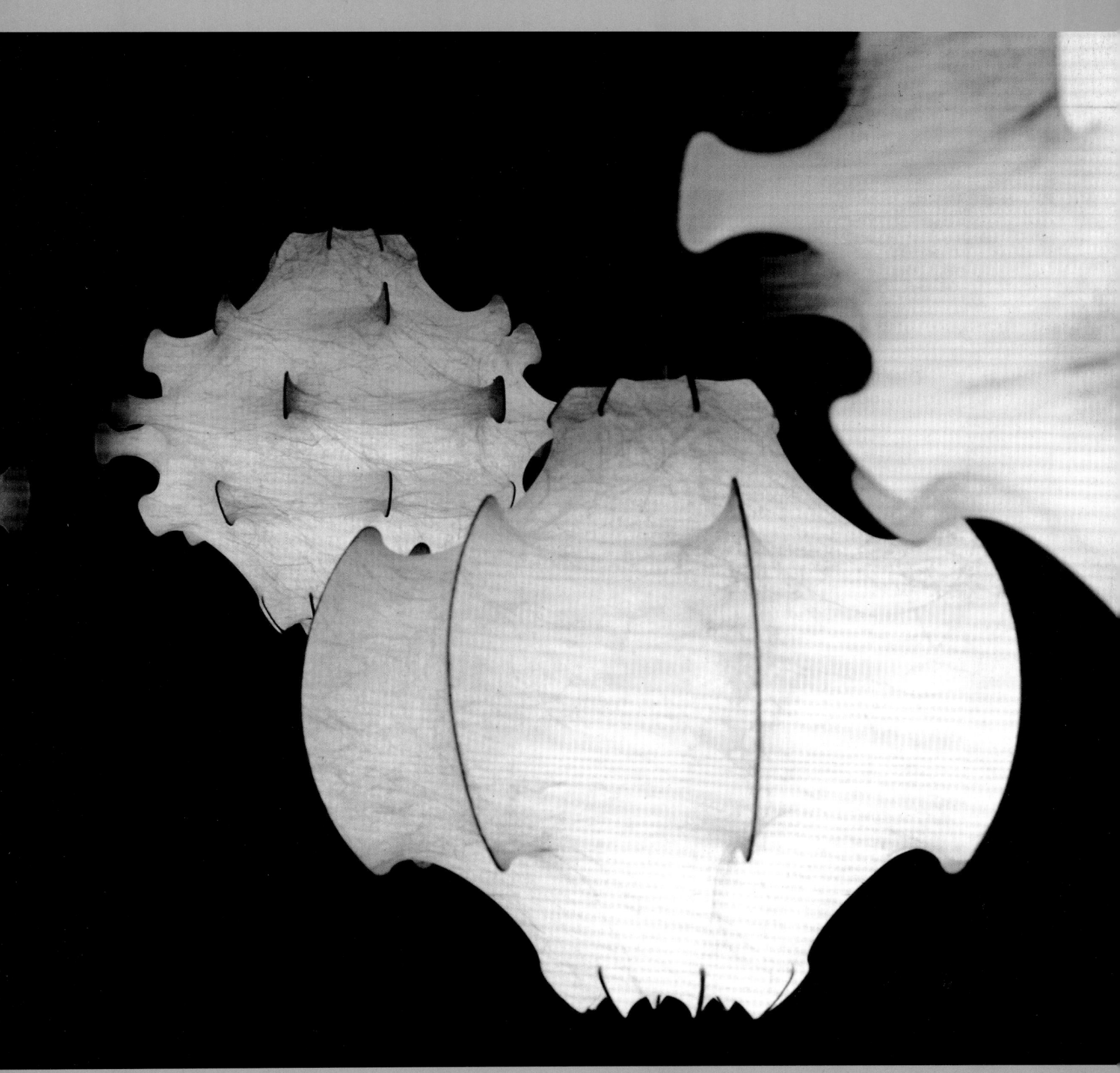

The Castiglioni Method

The Castiglioni studio was jointly founded by the two brothers Livio (1911-1979) and Pier Giacomo (1913-1968) in 1938. Initially Luigi Caccia Dominioni also contributed to the development of its projects. In 1944 Achille (1918-2002), the youngest of the brothers, who had just graduated in Architecture, joined the studio, although he had already started collaborating with them a few years earlier. Achille's creative partnership with Pier Giacomo (after Livio embarked on a parallel economic venture in 1952)[1] marked one of the most interesting and productive chapters in the history of Italian design from the point of view of the sharpness of ideas and the quality of work methods and planning—something the present books seeks to re-examine and introduce readers to.

These years witnessed "on the one hand the learned tradition of rationalist architecture, chiefly from Milan, to which the formal research of certain artistic groups was connected; and on the other an industrial culture, almost exclusively based in the north of Italy, which—with very few exceptions—was overall rather backward; caught between these stood a non-parcelled out labour force rooted in craftsmanship and still widespread throughout the country whose contribution in terms of ideas and creativeness has yet to be written."[2] This, in brief, are the conditions that led to the emergence of *Italian Design*, which the Castiglioni brothers rightfully belong to. It consists of a sort of complex design dimension capable of imbuing utensils, furnishings and house appliances, as well as vehicles, with the kind of formal, aesthetic and typologically creative surplus that makes Italian design famous throughout the world, especially thanks to the element of "taste" it intrinsically possesses and which is directly expressed by the appearance and image of every Italian-made product.

In this historical context, the Milan Triennale may serve as a useful "seismograph" to record the growth of industrial design in relation to architectural culture and on the fringes of the figurative artistic one. With the seventh edition of the Triennale, the year 1940 marked the official entrance of design into the world of Italian planning, alongside architecture and the decorative arts. The theme of the relation between furnishing and industrial production was directly approached by Giuseppe Pagano, the curator of the *Mostra internazionale della produzione di serie* (*International Serial Production Exhibition*), which documented the transformation of artisan workshops into factories for the serial production of universally reproducible models. While on the one hand this Triennale inevitably brought a comeback of the "literary" theme of the machine, on the other the concept of "standard" was developed, not merely as the technical-formal norm for the development of every industrial product, but also as a social and qualitative tool. The idea of standard became "the design principle capable of bringing all acts of interior décor development together through a methodological and ideal unity, a form of shared social ethos: 'from the spoon to the town', to quote the slogan used by Ernesto Nathan Rogers, which accompanied the culture of those years throughout the war period."[3] It was in the section devoted to radios at this edition of the Triennale that the brothers Livio and Pier Giacomo Castiglioni, together with Luigi Caccia Dominioni, first presented their five-valve 547 radio-receiver designed for Phonola. This object provides an embryonic illustration of the value and inventiveness of Italian design, based on the unique and lucky encounter between design and industry. It reveals a clear methodological leap: in the wake of the crucial radio-gramophone created by Figini and Pollini in 1933 and of Franco Albini's magical glass device from 1938, it transcended the idea of the radio as a piece of furniture, whereby technological devices were enclosed within wooden cases resembling bedside tables, dressers and period style pieces of furniture. The Castiglioni brothers did not camouflage their device so as to conceal it within furniture, but rather played on its affinity to the new technological objects. The 547 radio-receiver does not resemble a bedside table as much as a

Frisbi, hanging lamp designed by Achille Castiglioni and manufactured by Flos, 1978

telephone; its central and upturned sound diffuser looks like a microphone. "It was the first radio-receiver to have a plastic casing that was not intended to imitate previous wooden radio-cabinets, but which sought instead to invent a new form for an object that had changed with technology."[4] The modes and qualities of use of the object were redeveloped from an "integral" perspective, which is to say in close connection to the possibility of manufacturing its components and rationalizing their arrangement. This first design feat already illustrated certain points of reference destined to become recurrent features in the Castiglioni brothers' work in years to follow, namely: "the challenging of the type of object to be designed and of its function within space (the new radio they designed could be rested on a surface as well as suspended), and an anti-rhetorical and affectionate use of items, based on an apparent downplaying of their importance in terms of expression, combined with a desire to equip objects with the radical quality of everyday, timeless utensils."[5] What we find is a procedure that mitigated the iconoclastic rigour of the rationalism of the previous decade, fostering a freer form of design, no longer confined by pre-established and ideological truths. Keeping somewhat aloof, perhaps, from the themes of physical and civil reconstruction in the aftermath of the Second World War, the Castiglioni brothers developed a method of work and research that on the one hand was rooted in functionalism, but on the other was linked to the pragmatism of the period. To this they added a good dose of irony and inventiveness, an interest towards humble and traditional models, and a willingness to "rediscover" anonymous objects, which they would break down according to materials, components and methods of manufacture. The serial furniture section which hosted the work of the Castiglioni brothers at the 8th Triennale of 1949—the year in which they also took part in the 14th national radio exhibition—illustrated the designers' belief that certain traditional chairs of unknown craftsmanship could be of interest not only from the point of view of the renewal of style, but also because they possessed an intrinsic modernness which "simply" needed to be brought out, in order to test the possibility of applying the new methods of serial production to the objects. What we have here is an outline of the concept of *redesign*, the observation of everyday objects and investigation of "the form of the useful" which was destined to lead the Castiglioni brothers towards the development of a procedure codified in all of its necessary varieties. "Having identified—through a penetrating structural interpretation—a salient performance core in traditional furnishings and utilitarian objects, [the Castiglioni brothers] measured themselves up against the risk of enriching it with a subtle yet noticeable acceleration on the level of communication as well."[6] This work process lies at the basis of pieces such as the trestle tables Leonardo and Bramante (1950), which are still being manufactured by Zanotta—proof of the value of a project that was destined to withstand the test of time.

At the 10th Triennale of 1954 industrial design still played a leading role thanks to the *Congresso Internazionale dell'Industrial Design* (International Congress of Industrial Design)—where alongside technicians, architects and designers Enzo Paci had invited philosophers, writers and critics—as well as the *Mostra dell'industrial design* (the Industrial Design Exhibition curated by the Castiglioni brothers, M. Nizzoli and A. Morello, among others). The latter event was excellently planned by the Castiglioni brothers and Michele Provinciali, who presented 150 objects chosen from the leading examples of world industrial design. Among the distinguishing features of the exhibit was the prominent and well-established presence of Scandinavian, German and British products; the evaluation of the concept of design as "the problem of form in the industrial manufacturing process, constituting a fundamental point of encounter between art and industry"; and finally the affirmation of Italian *Bel Design*. Alongside this international exhibit others were organized—on "The Idea of Standard", "The

The Gavina shop, Milan, designed by Achille
and Pier Giacomo Castiglioni, 1962

RAI exhibit pavilion at the 43rd Fair of Milan, "The Spread of
the Radio and Television in Country Towns", project by Achille
and Pier Giacomo Castiglioni, visual layout by Enzo Mari, 1965

pp. 28-29
10th Triennale of Milan, the mounting
and arranging of the "Industrial Design
Section", project by Achille e Pier Giacomo
Castiglioni, 1954

Home", and "Individual Pieces of Furniture"—revealing the tendency of Italian design to focus on the domestic landscape. It was on this occasion that the young furniture manufacturer Dino Gavina first grasped the role of Milan as the city of innovation in the field of design. Lucio Fontana got him into the 10th Triennale, so that he could meet the brothers Pier Giacomo and Achille Castiglioni, as well as Carlo Scarpa and Luigi Caccia Dominioni, with whom he was later to produce some of the most important pieces in the history of Italian design. This professional and creative partnership between architects and manufacturers is what lies at the basis of the success and spread of Italian design across the world, as a specific expression of the Italian furniture industry. Under different guises this link has endured over time, passing on its underlying approach and the quality of its design down to the present day, engaging generations of professionals with the most diverse personalities and expressive languages. The encounter between architects and manufacturers—as well as that between the "utopian" drives and creative freedom of architects and designers on the one hand and the role of art directors assigned to them by companies on the other, where design expertise would meet openness to innovation—enabled the pursuit of actual experimental research in the field of furnishing in the 1950s and 60s: "the collaboration between designers and producers has been a constant matter of debate right from the beginning of industrial serial production, and hence of so-called industrial design. The history of design is dotted with traces of the development of this collaboration, which so far has proven fundamental for companies' success."[7]
On the same occasion, an area "parallel" to architectural planning and industrial design clearly emerged, a field for experimental research and testing which first the Castiglioni brothers and later Achille alone were to resolutely develop: the mounting of exhibits. The large suspended disks and striking backlit screens that marked the room for the Industrial Design section of the 10th Trien-

nale provided an occasion to approach light as a "compositional material". It was perhaps in the field of exhibits, more than in that of design, that the Castiglioni brothers attained "the greatest experimental freedom […] or rather the greatest possibility to infringe the methodological rules for the construction of industrial objects which they had set themselves. [The exhibits of] these years [took the form of a] series of exceptions and experiments, whose figurative and technical materials to a large extent flowed into their work as designers in later years."[8]
The "pyrotechnic" exhibits in the RAI pavilion at the Fair of Milan (between 1952 and 1970) may be viewed as "exercises in style" which, following the narrative example set by Raymond Queneau's famous book (*Exercises de Style*, 1947), redescribed the same "theme" in compositional and architectural terms according to different modes and approaches.

Flos Showroom, Milan, project by Achille Castiglioni, 1984

Later, by contrast, following the demolition of the original pavilion, it was temporary projects that served as environmental opportunities as well as "simple venues" where to exhibit products—venues conceived as areas of interaction between the public and the operators, mutually engaged through the solutions adopted in terms of architecture and means of communication. This itinerary across the world of exhibits unfolded over the course of the years, leading to Achille Castiglioni's projects for BTicino (1985-1999), which were approached from the perspective of "micro-town-planning."[9]

When it comes to industrial design, Rem's portable shoulder vacuum cleaner Spalter (1956) and the five-valve Phonola radio remain crucial examples of the reinvention—in terms of both typology and material—of household appliances conceived "on a serial scale". Another central theme, and not merely for the Triennale, was that of homes and furnishings, which through a single and synergic planning action combined the designing of objects and furniture with the definition, if not of specific spaces, at least of ideas for inhabitable spaces. In July 1957 the exhibition 'Colori e forme nella casa d'oggi' ('Colours and Shapes in Today's Home') was inaugurated in Villa Olmo in Como. In their furnished room here Achille and Pier Giacomo Castiglioni presented a programme based on the mingling of historical and contemporary elements, which defied the assumptions of rationalism by replacing the geometrical rigour of "abstract spaces" with a complex form of modernity, defined not so much by architectural preconceptions as by values such as the freedom of choice, precariousness and accidentalness. The Castiglioni brothers' brilliant *bricolage*—a room with a terracotta floor and wooden windows with internal shutters—dialectically and "spontaneously" combined designed pieces and "anonymous" ones, while a television hanging from the ceiling engaged with a period painting. A painted decoration by Giuseppe Ajmone instead emphasized the need to create a link between design and contemporary painting. Yet another idea of domestic space and of the engagement between new furniture design and "pre-existing environmental elements on a private scale" is to be found in the theme explored by the Castiglioni brothers for the exhibition 'La casa abitata' ('The Inhabited House', curated by G. Michelucci and P.G. Spadolini, among others). This was held in Palazzo Strozzi in Florence in 1965. The exhibition for the first time provided a structured configuration of "inhabited" environments, furnished with contemporary designer pieces. The Castiglioni brothers, Magistretti, Sottsass, Ricci, Gregotti and Stoppino all sought to define a possible "system for home living" alternative to the one based on "period furniture", which dominated the market. Some of the design suggestions verged on a synthesis between interior architecture and furnishings, which were merged to provide a single plastic and compositional solution. Aside from these aspects, others emerged connected to the "way" of inhabiting a house: "this exhibition was intended to bring out those characteristics that an average inhabited house takes on when unexpected elements—necessary ones or which the family members like—are superimposed upon a pre-established order, thus engendering discontinuity and contradictions, if only apparently. For on top of the underlying and pre-established instrumentation of a house there is the sentimental stratification created by furnishings, personal objects and the emotional and cultural background, which make the house inhabited" (from the report issued by the Organizing Committee).

Achille and Pier Giacomo Castiglioni, architects and designers "who entered the Hall of Fame of outstanding 20th-century designers [make up] a crucial chapter in any history of contemporary design, [delineating] a figure that appears to be in its obvious place, yet at the same time is ill at ease."[10] The Castiglioni brothers remain a point of reference for Italian design not so much for their "style" as for their work—which must be grasped in all of its complexity—and for their "method". The extraordinary planning, aesthetic and crea-

tive partnership between the two brothers has led to the creation of a boundless series of exhibits, interiors, architectures, furnishings and utilitarian objects through an in-depth exploration of each type. New types were also invented by anticipating certain ideas and utility objects, revealing the full weight of a "complex, crossover and multifaceted kind of design characterized by approaches and methodologies which can hardly be confined to individual professions, whose boundaries they tend to transcend. [This approach to design and untiring research may be seen as] an attempt to express an original synthesis between experimental flight and rational planning, […] visual ideas […] and a playful drive, […] the baffling play of some of (their) best creations, where the measure determined by reason through cruel and subdued cheerfulness is combined with the estranging disorientation caused by the sudden discovery it forces one to make."[11]

The Castiglioni brothers first and then Achille alone—after Pier Giacomo passed away—led this "clever game" in the best possible way. Their shared itinerary unfolded from 1938 down to the late 1960s, while continuing into the new millennium through Achille's work, which appears closely connected to the teaching and definition of a method, expressing the endurance of a valuable and uncommon sensitivity. The results achieved in terms of projects—in the fields of both exhibits and design—still appear striking on account of their creativeness, incisiveness, elegance and formal perfection. They remain points of reference for all designers and for anyone wishing to approach the history of design and exhibits in post-war Italy. "Redesign"—as already mentioned, a design practice which led to the creation of the Lierna chair (1960 for Gavina) as a brilliant Art Nouveau reinvention, of a domestic version of urban flower stalls, and later of the foldable three-legged table Cumano (1977, for Zanotta), a bistrot piece of furniture brought into people's homes—and "readymade" are two concepts crucial to the Castiglioni "method". This is illustrated by objects such as the Toio floor lamp (1962), comprised of a car headlight mounted on a thin stem of drawn chromed metal equipped with fishing-rod loops through which the electric wire runs; the amazing Mezzadro (1957), a spare yet perfect stool consisting of a tractor seat in perforated metal; and, last but not least, the Sella seat (1957), a clever invention which enables one to sit on a rocking "Brooks" bicycle leather saddle supported by a stem fixed to a hemispherical base. These are objects of design which have become classic models transcending the notion of style and all trends thanks to their enduring value.

To these we should add other ingenious inventions from the point of view of matter and composition, such as the Sanluca armchair (1960, for Gavina, but now newly released by Poltrona Frau). This is like the timeless symbol of a dynamic and innovative form of design. Almost reminiscent of Boccioni's sculpture, it anticipated serial assembly techniques in its components. It was a fixture ready for the assembly line of a furniture industry which had not yet reached maturity and was still developing. The Splügen Bräu lamp (1960) was especially designed for the Milanese restaurant by this name, thus once again emphasizing the link between design and architecture. Taccia (1962) and Luminator (1957) are spare lighting devices that anticipated minimalist design by forty years; Taraxacum (1960), again produced for Flos, was the last lamp made from a foam intended to protect the vehicles transported on military ships from adverse weather conditions and especially salinity. Once sprayed on the metal-wire supporting structure, this foam would turn into a solid and resistant material layer. This illustrates how the creative "shift" in the "correct" way of using a given material could become an "invention", enabling the manufacturing of a series of suspended and lighting objects, including the smaller Viscontea and Gatto lamps (1960). The Arco floor lamp (1962), a kind of ingenious domestic version of a street lamp, reflects an idea of freedom in the use of space, enabling users to shine light from above in every corner of the house without having to worry about any formal ranking among rooms or the central lighting points conventionally arranged by sellers in every apartment.

Many other objects ought to be mentioned to commemorate the inexhaustible creative outburst and professional and critical success characterizing the partnership between the Castiglioni brothers in the 1960s and leading to Achille's creations, which extended from the following decade to the turn of the millennium. These were in perfect compliance with the "Castiglioni method", which never flagged, but on the contrary always preserved an extraordinary vital strength.

The "smiling expressionism" of the Castiglioni brothers is a method which may be summed up through a series of programme-slogans of reference: while invoking the lapidary concept "function, what a nice form", almost ten years ago Achille Castiglioni gave the following answer to the question "How does one become a good designer?": "If you're not curious, give up. If you're not interested in other people, in what they do and how they act, then the designer's life is not for you. Good projects spring not from the ambition to leave one's mark, but from the will to establish an exchange, even a small exchange, with the unknown person who will be using the object you have designed. Rest assured that research is everything and that each individual object produced is simply a stage and temporary stop rather than an ending. […] The aim of the designer is not to ideologize false memories, but to convey messages of curiosity, enjoyment and affection to other people."

On the occasion of an exhibition held at the New York MoMA in the late 1990s, Stefano Casciani quite rightly described Achille Castiglioni as the "President of the Republic of Design". He and his brother Pier Giacomo— "two bodies, a single head"[12]—are now remembered as two "brilliant minds who worked through synthesis, competence and experience: the real stars and circus athletes of Italian design" (Alessandro Mendini).

Notes

[1] For a critical historical overview of Livio Castiglioni's work, see D. Scodeller, *Livio e Piero Castiglioni – Il progetto della luce*, Milan: Electa, 2003.
[2] G. Bosoni and A. Nulli, "Italia: storie parallele tra progetto e consumo", in Various Authors, *Storia del disegno industriale-1919-1990 il dominio del design*, Milan: Electa, 1991.
[3] V. Gregotti, *Il disegno del prodotto industriale. Italia 1860-1980*, Milan: Electa, 1982.
[4] A. Castiglioni, "Dialogo con Achille Castiglioni", in *Achille Castiglioni, Franco Sbarro. Esperienze di architettura: generazioni a confronto*, Quaderni dell'Accademia di architettura di Mendrisio, Skira, without date.
[5] V. Gregotti, "Traviamenti interpretativi", in P. Ferrari and A. Castiglioni, *Achille Castiglioni*, Milan: Electa, 1984.
[6] S. Polano, *Castiglioni tutte le opere 1938-2000*, Milan: Electa, 2001.
[7] P. Antonelli, in G. Castelli, P. Antonelli and F. Pichi, *La fabbrica del design – Conversazioni con i protagonisti del design italiano*, Milan: Skira, 2007.
[8] V. Gregotti, "Traviamenti interpretativi", *cit.*
[9] See S. Casciani, "Allestimento come Urbanistica", in *Achille Castiglioni per BTicino*, Pubblicazione di BTicino, without date.
[10] S. Polano, *op.cit.*
[11] *Ibid.*
[12] D. Buzzati, "Un grande designer", in *Corriere della Sera*, 3 December 1968, p.3.

❝ ...I cannot but wish that education and culture will lead users to reject prestige pieces, and the industry to manufacture increasingly genuine and less expensive objects, without using designers' names to raise the prices. Let designers' names disappear but their works be used, if valuable, to create products of real industrial design—ones that can be labelled neither Italian nor European. So: not Italian success, but the success of a valuable design method. **❞**

(*The Designer Is Not a Fanciful Artist*, conference by Achille Castiglioni in Courtray, 19 October 1970)

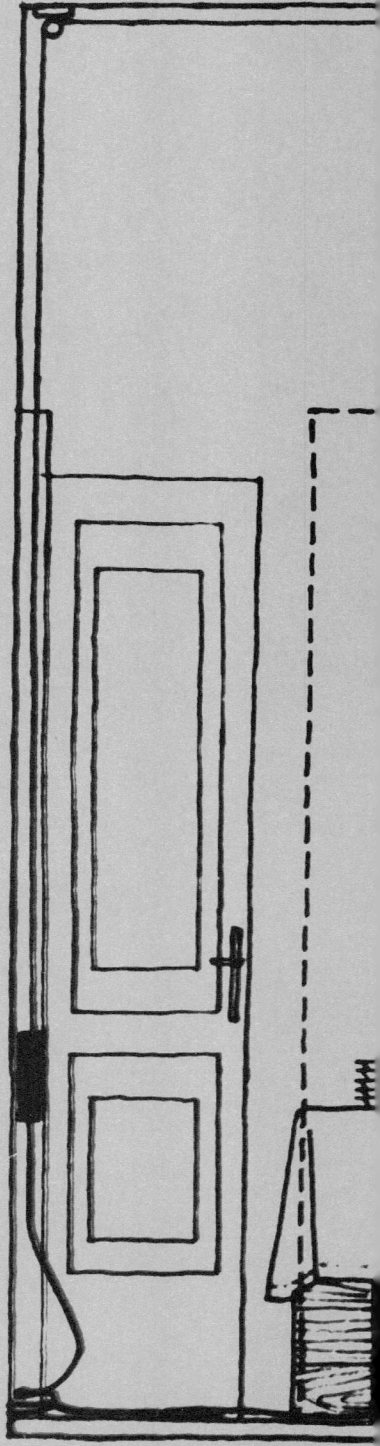

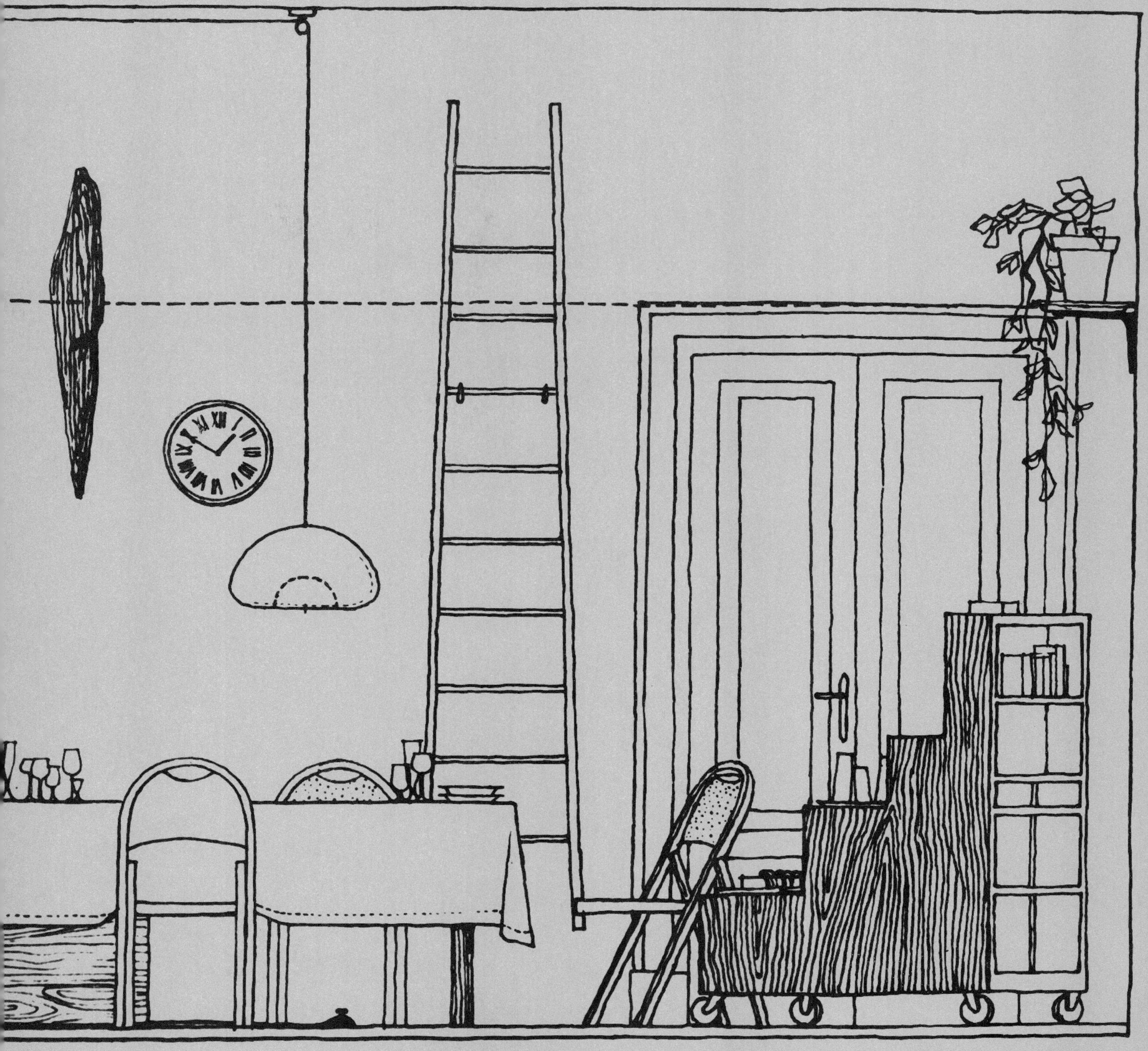

Catalogue of Objects

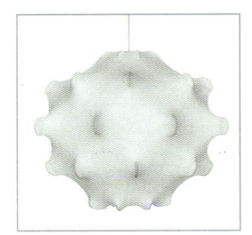

TARAXACUM 60

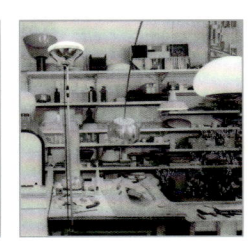

SPLÜGEN BRÄU

THE CASTIGLIONI STUDIO

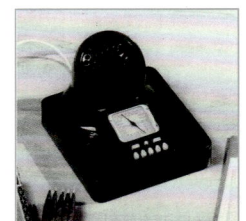

THE 547 RADIO-RECEIVER

LUMINATOR

SELLA

THE SPLÜGEN BRÄU BEERHOUSE

ARCO

SERVI

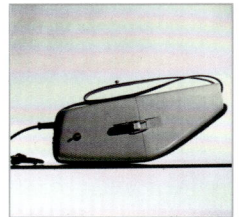

1940 – 1950   1960

SPALTER

MEZZADRO

SANLUCA

TOIO

TACCIA

PHOTO-CAMERA

TARAXACUM 88

SNOOPY

ACETOLIERE

RAMPA 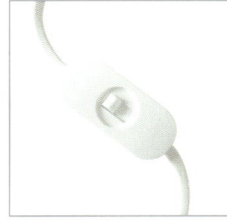 | SINGLE-POLE IN-LINE SWITCH 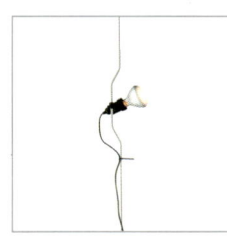 | PARENTESI  | DRY  | BAVERO  | JOY

1970 - 1980 - 1990

MAYONNAISE SPOON  | RR126  | CUMANO  | GIBIGIANA  | BRERA  | FRUIT BOWL/COLANDER

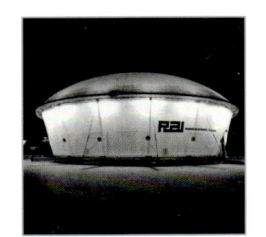

RAI TENSILE STRUCTURE  | PRIMATE  | 5C  | DIABOLO

TELEPHONE

37

The Objects

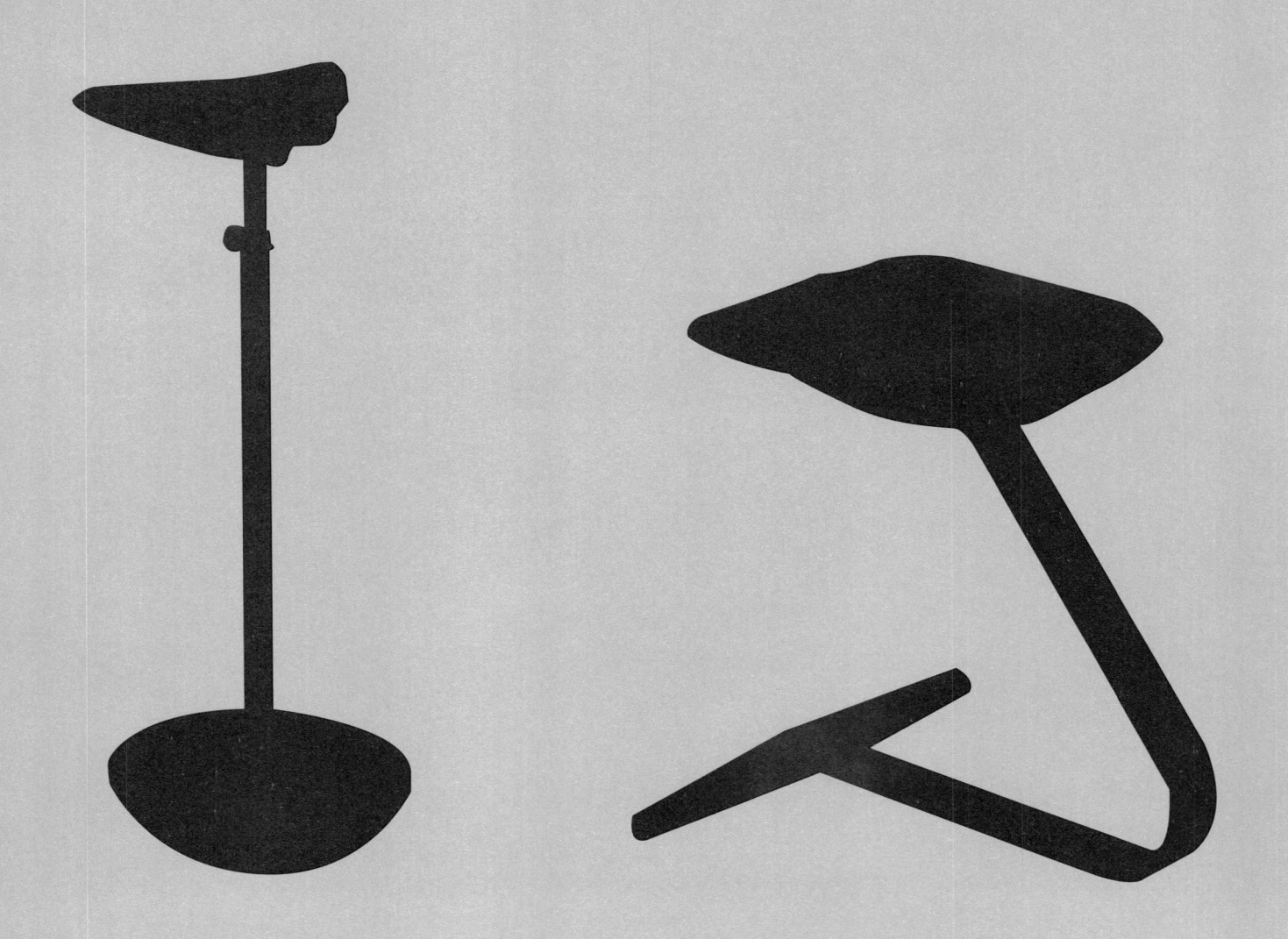

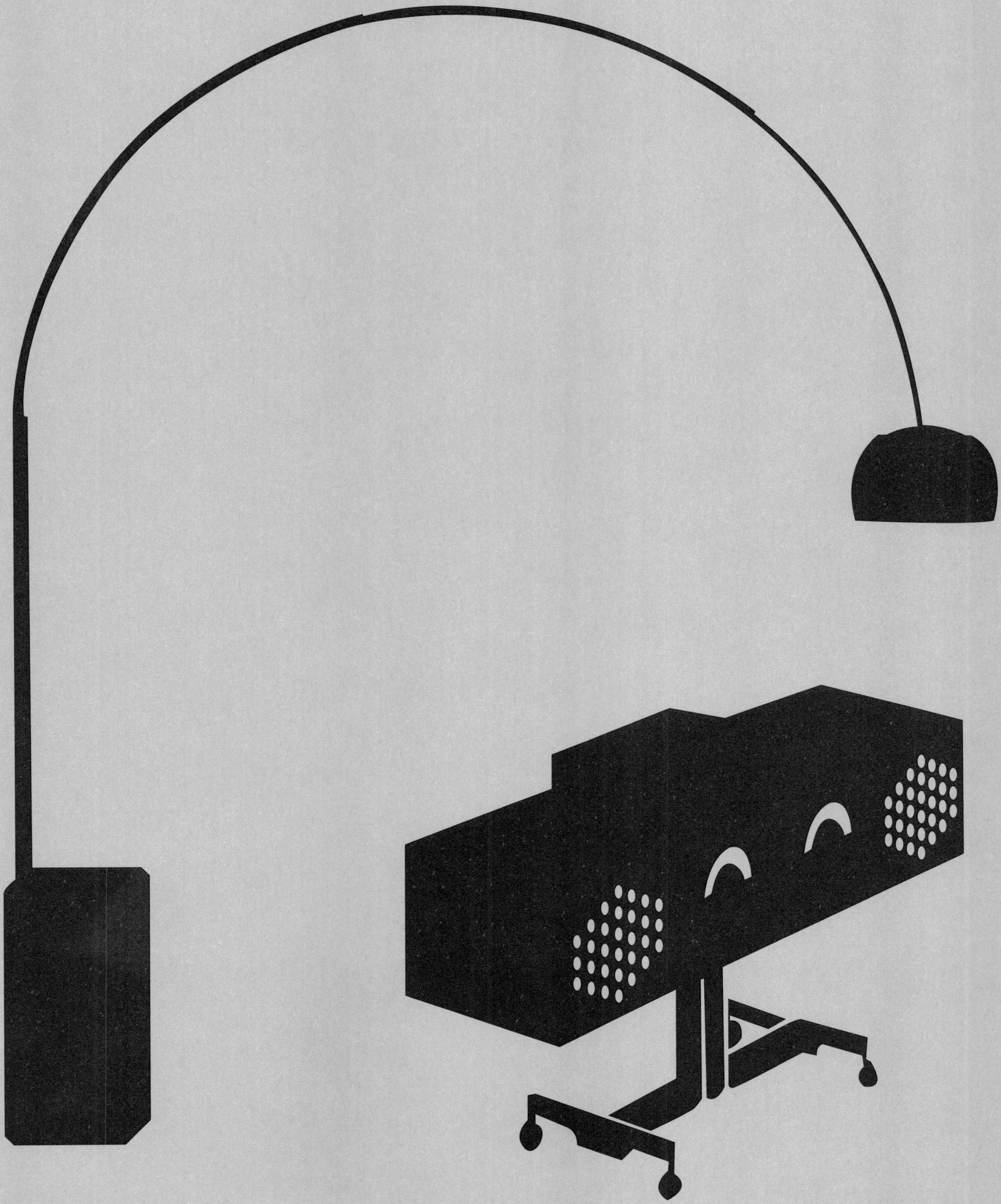

FIVE-VALVE 547 RADIO-RECEIVER

Designers: Livio and Pier Giacomo Castiglioni, Luigi Caccia Dominioni

Year: 1940

Company: Phonola

Materials: bakelite outer shell

At the 7th Milan Triennale of 1940, in the section devoted to radios, the brothers Livio and Pier Giacomo Castiglioni, together with Luigi Caccia Dominioni, presented the five-valve 547 radio-receiver they had designed for Phonola. This object provides an embryonic illustration of the value and inventiveness of Italian design, as well as the unique and lucky encounter between planning and industry. It reveals a clear methodological leap: in the wake of the crucial radio-gramophone created by Figini and Pollini in 1933 and of Franco Albini's magical glass device from 1938, it transcended the idea of the radio as a piece of furniture, whereby technological devices were enclosed within wooden cases resembling bedside tables, dressers and period style pieces of furniture. To quote the designers themselves, "the radio-receiver must be a 'device' first and foremost, a machine, if we like, or a tool; once again, we should turn to objects like telephones, typewriters, pianos and radiators, where all the components, including the protective casing, are only intended to serve a given function: so much so, that the word 'furniture' has never cropped up in relation to them."

The Castiglioni brothers did not camouflage their device so as to conceal it within furniture, but rather played on its affinity to the new technological objects. The 547 radio-receiver does not resemble a bedside table as much as a telephone, with control keys located on the small panel at the centre; its central and upturned sound diffuser looks like a microphone. "It was the first radio-receiver to have have a plastic casing that was not intended to imitate previous wooden radio-cabinets, but which sought instead to invent a new form for an object that had changed with technology" (Achille Castiglioni).

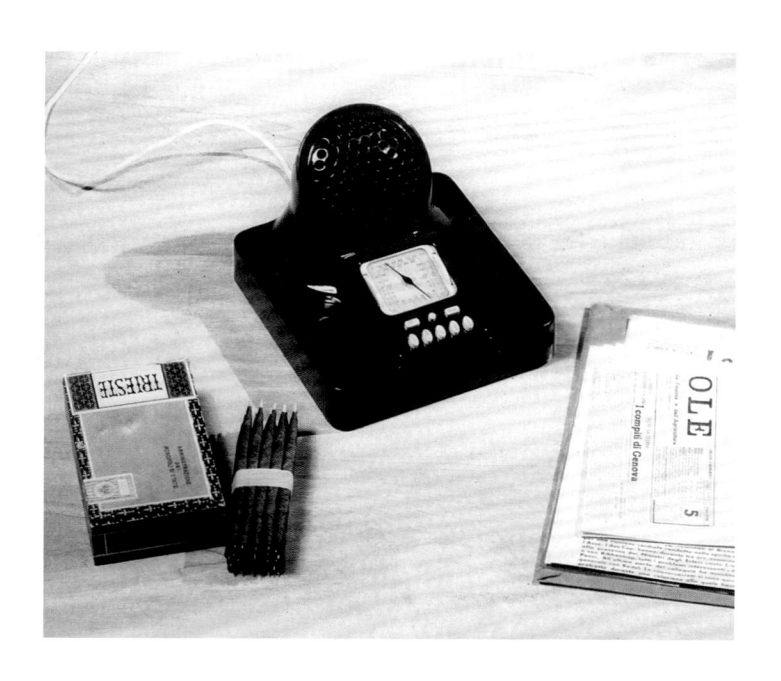

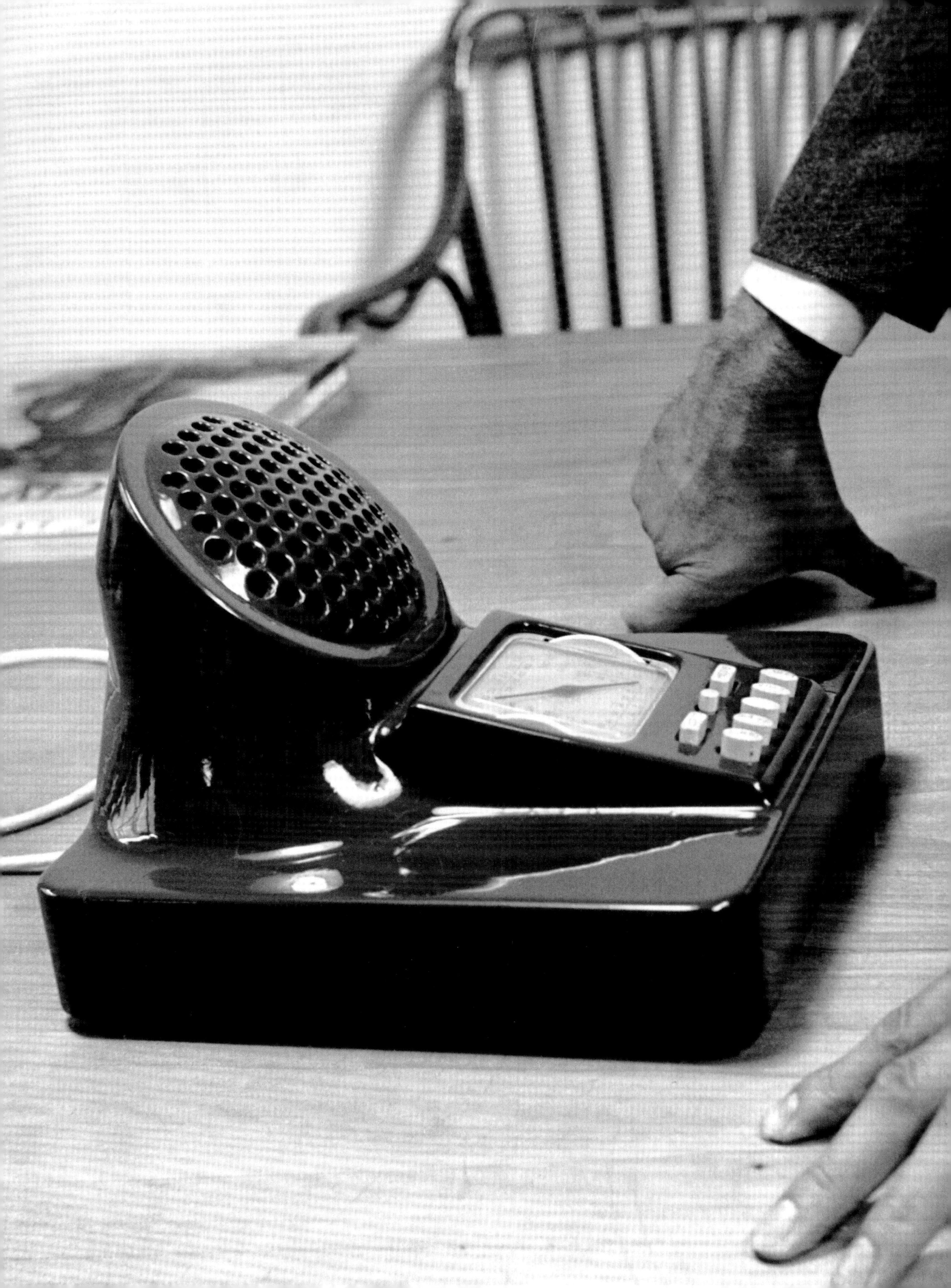

LUMINATOR

Designers: Achille and Pier Giacomo Castiglioni

Year: 1955

Company: Gilardi & Barzaghi, Artform (1957), Flos (1994)

Materials: floor lamp providing indirect lighting, stem consisting of an aluminium tube painted various colours, supporting metal rods

Compasso d'Oro Award 1955

Through his timeless Luminator lamp (1933) Pietro Chiesa made an attempt to develop a domestic version of the kind of indirect lighting used in photography studios. The Castiglioni brothers paid explicit homage to this object by designing a floor lamp bearing the same name, which was awarded the Compasso d'Oro in 1955. Originally designed for this competition, where it was among the winners, the Castiglioni brothers' Luminator served—in their own words—to provide "an answer to the demand for a 'form of the useful' for Italian industry." Intended to be industrially manufactured, this lamp is comprised of just a few essential components: a stem consisting of a coloured aluminium tube enclosing the lamp socket; three legs consisting of rods that may be unscrewed and inserted inside the stem itself for transport convenience; and a silver bulb directing the light upwards and which requires no side screens, as the lighting source is already screened. The minimal and spare form given to the object—almost a graphic mark turned into a lamp—and the attention paid to the lighting source's engineering characteristics as an initial stimulus make this lamp a forerunner of contemporary minimalism.

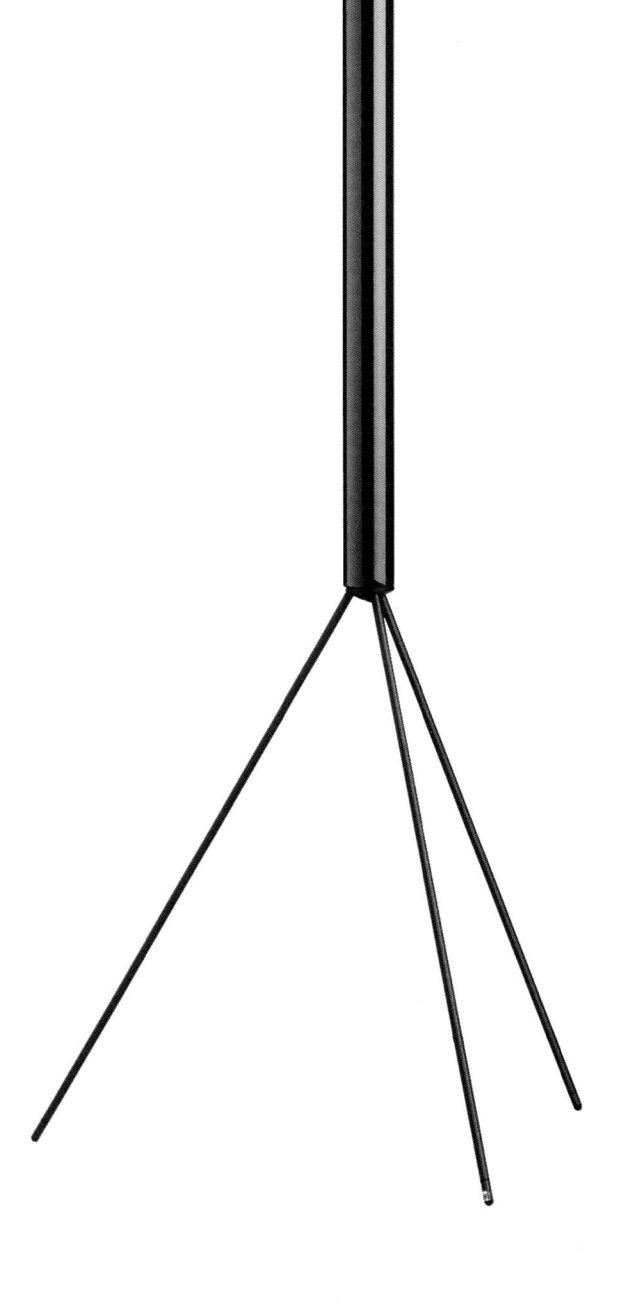

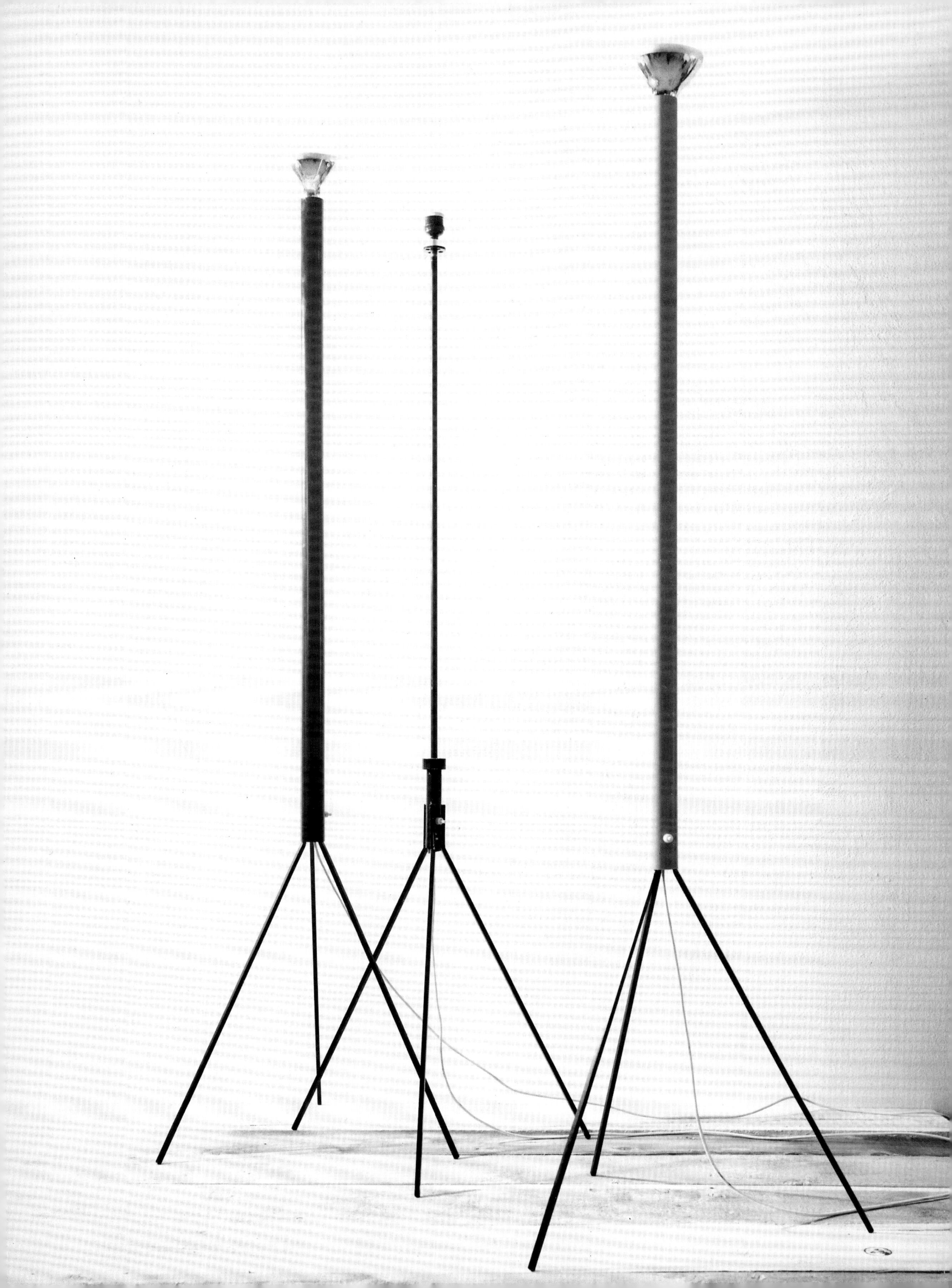

SPALTER

Designers: **Achille and Pier Giacomo Castiglioni**

Year: **1956**

Company: **Rem**

Materials: **vacuum cleaner, nylon shell, adjustable leather shoulder strap**

"I made my first contact with a large-scale industry through Rem, for the designing of a vacuum cleaner" (Achille Castiglioni). As a project, Spalter showed Italian industrial design the path it was to follow: that of engagement with companies and of a conceptual synergy in the creation of objects, so the latter would spring from an agreement and partnership between designers and businessmen. In its name, Spalter combines the ideas of shoulder (Italian "spalla") and ground ("terra") use. It was an innovative object both for its formal attributions, based on the pursuit of miniaturization, and for its choice of materials. The small vacuum cleaner is comprised of two shells made of nylon (a flexible and shatter-proof thermoplastic material ensuring a high level of electric insulation)—one enclosing the engine and fan, the other a dust filter. Shaped like a backpack, Spalter could be used either by carrying it through a shoulder strap or by more conventionally dragging it on the floor. The sled-like shape of its shell and the presence of a small felt dish attached to its front fissure made it easy to move the vacuum cleaner across the floor even without any wheels.

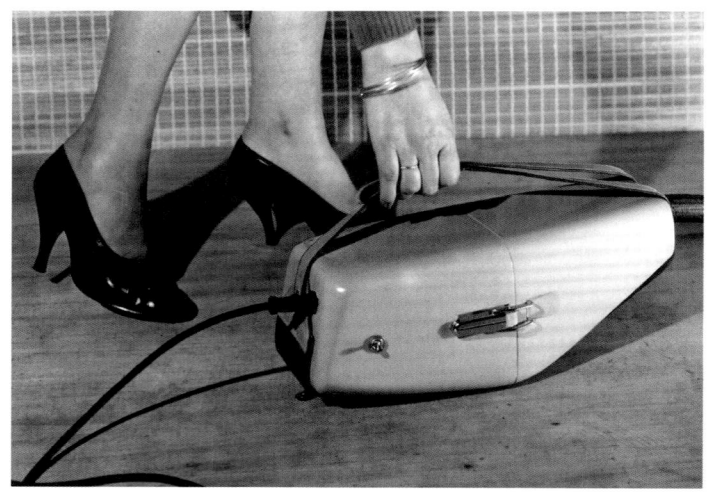

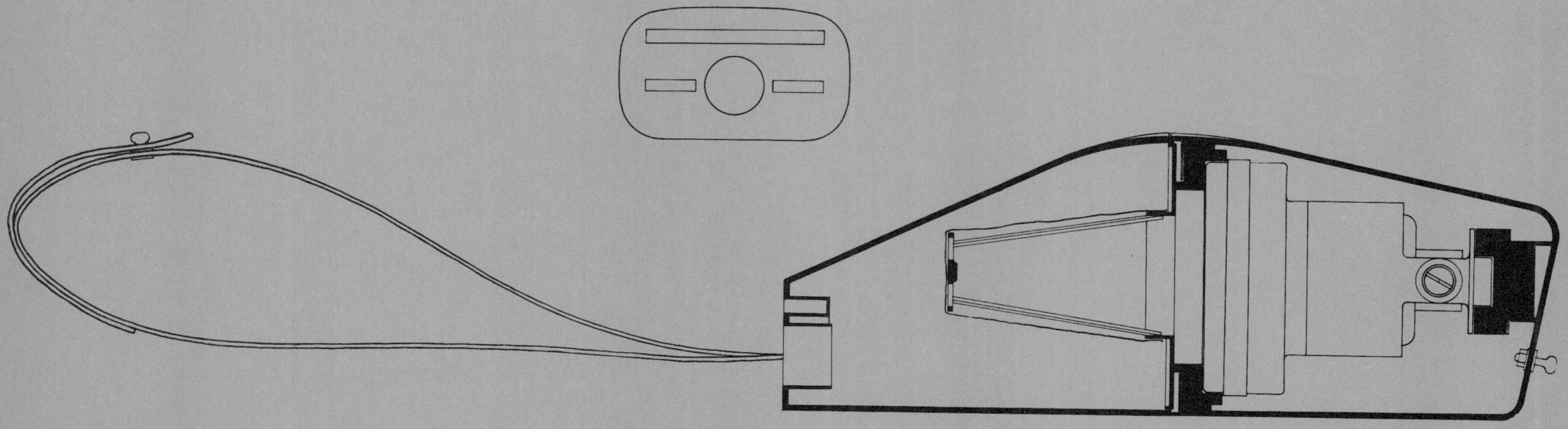

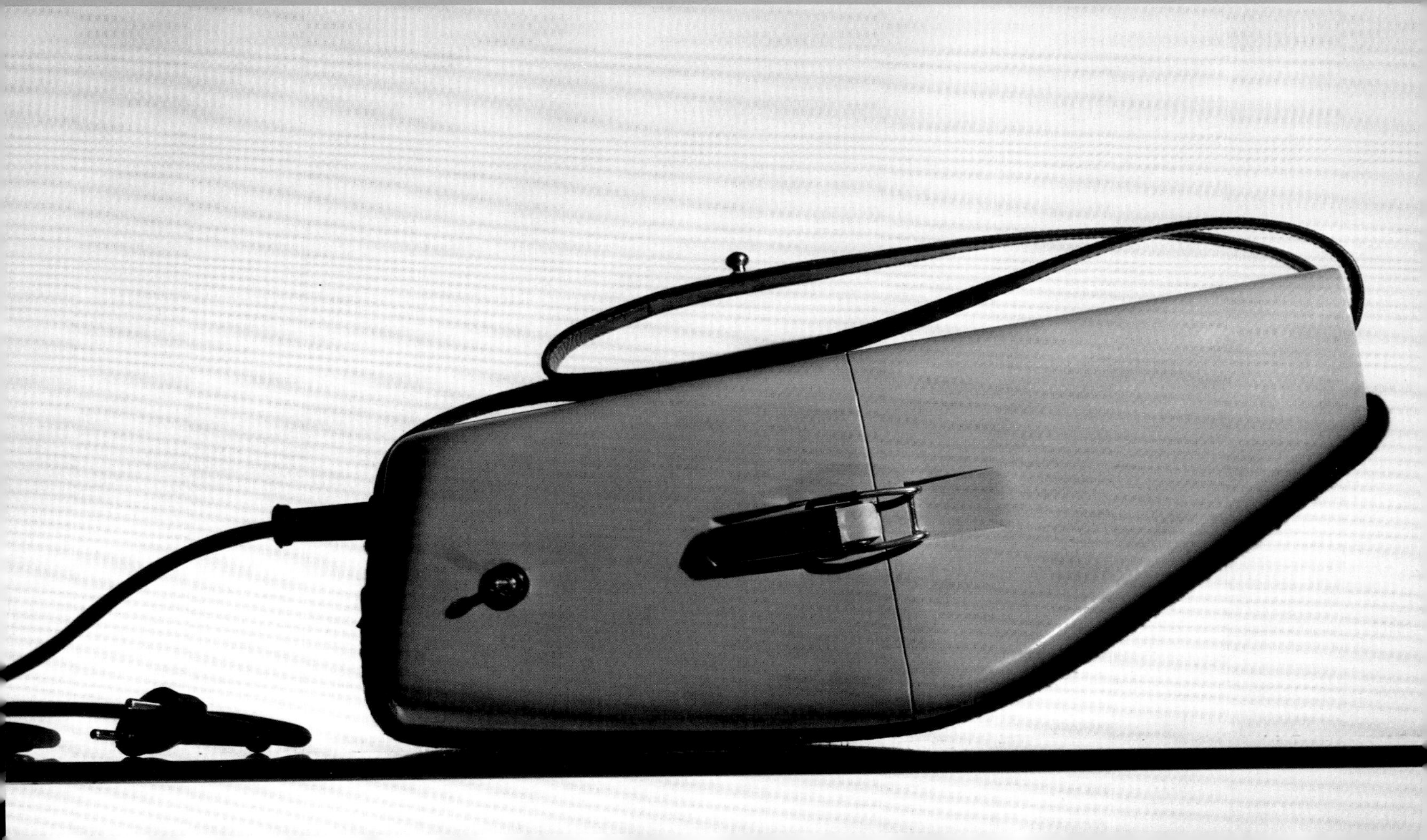

'COLORI E FORME DELLA CASA D'OGGI' EXHIBITION

Planners: Achille and Pier Giacomo Castiglioni

Year: 1957

In July 1957 the exhibition 'Colori e forme nella casa d'oggi' ('Colours and Shapes in Today's Home') was inaugurated in Villa Olmo in Como. In their furnished room here Achille and Pier Giacomo Castiglioni presented a programme based on the mingling of historical and contemporary elements—something already foreshadowed by Franco Albini's domestic interiors—which defied the assumptions of rationalism by replacing the geometrical rigour of "abstract spaces" with a complex form of modernity, defined not so much by architectural preconceptions as by values such as the freedom of choice, precariousness, accidentalness, and engagment. The Castiglioni brothers' brilliant "inhabitable bricolage"—a space with a terracotta floor and wooden windows with internal shutters—dialectically and "spontaneously" combined designed pieces and "anonymous" ones, while a television hanging from the ceiling engaged with a period painting. A painted stencil decoration executed by Giuseppe Ajmone ran along the walls, broken off by a small enamelled cast iron sink, of the kind used in Milanese courtyards. This artistic touch emphasized the need to create a link between design and contemporary painting. This proposed living room featured the prototypes of pieces destined to endure as icons of the "Castiglioni method": the Mezzadro stool (1957), consisting of a tractor seat in perforated metal attached to a supporting structure, and the Sella rocking stool (1957), comprised of a bicycle saddle fixed to a vertical pink tube. As Achille Castiglioni explained: "the room one lives in, the living room, must be made using the things needed to inhabit it, without any prearranged planning, but paying attention to the way in which things are used." In the typological stratification and mingling of ordinary objects and design we find a willingness to engage with history and the inexhaustible repository of everyday items which in Villa Olmo the Castiglioni brothers presented as their foundational and research programme for the years to come.

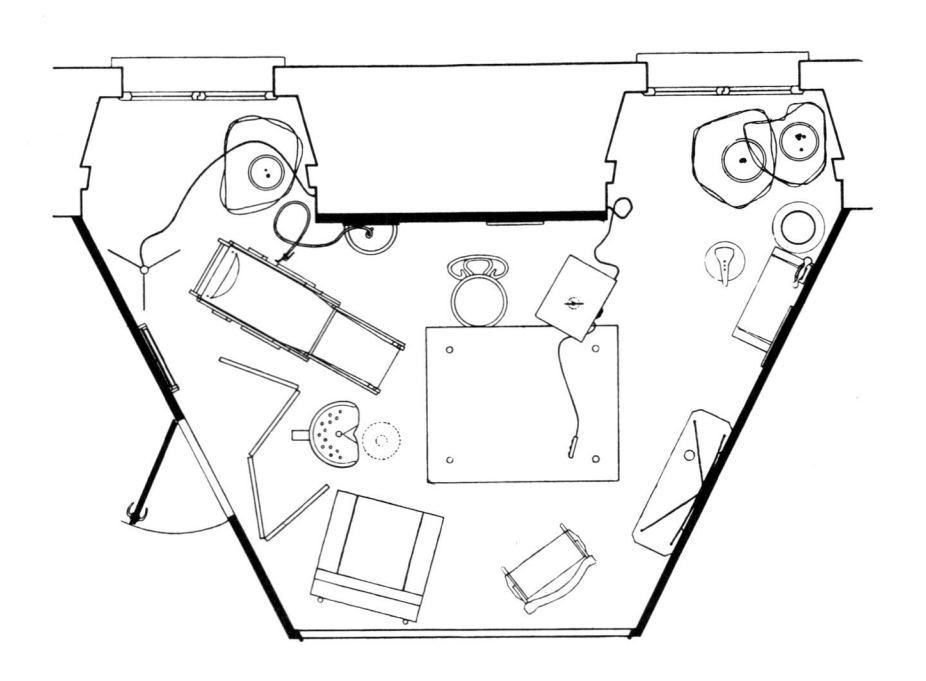

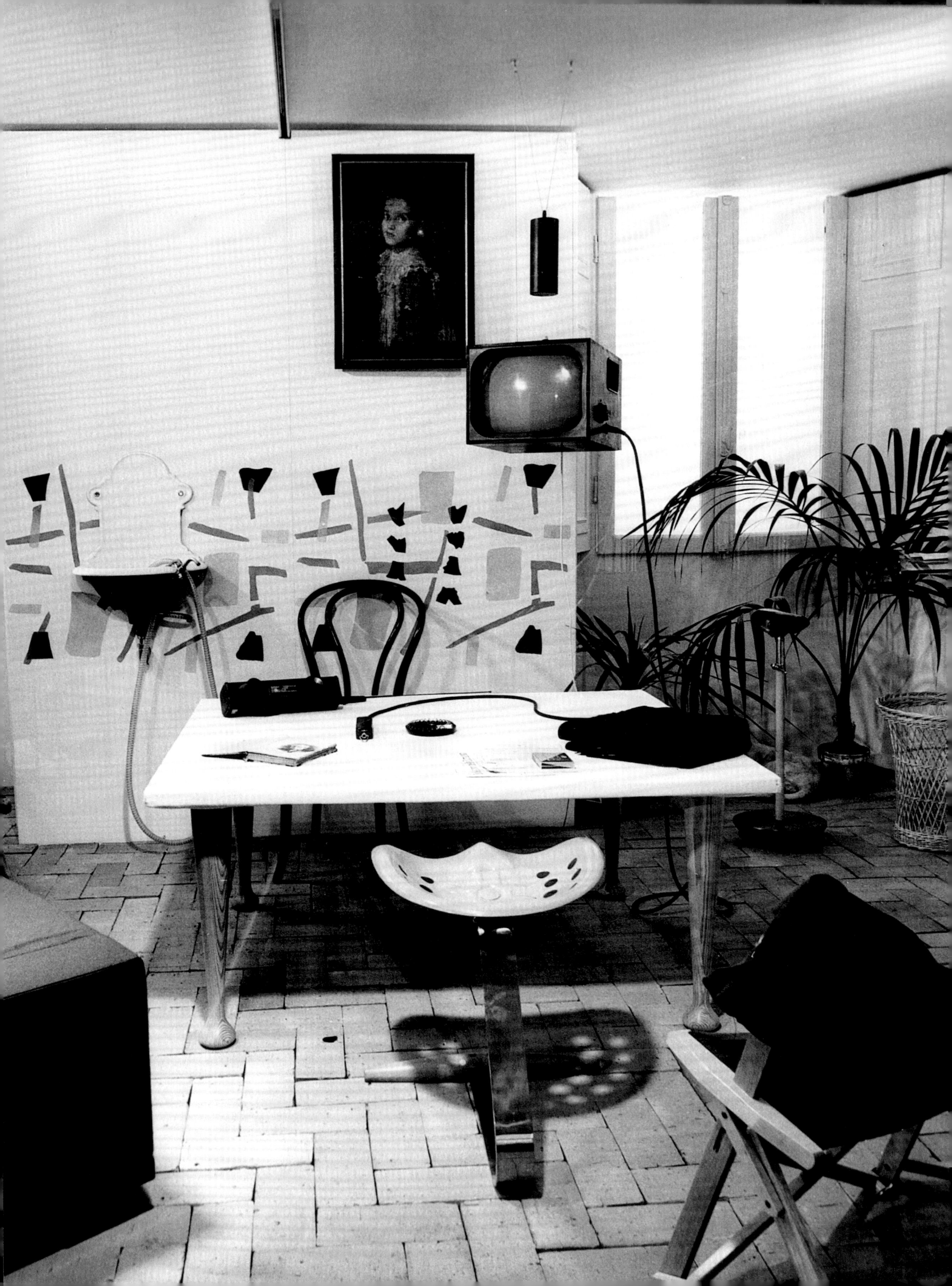

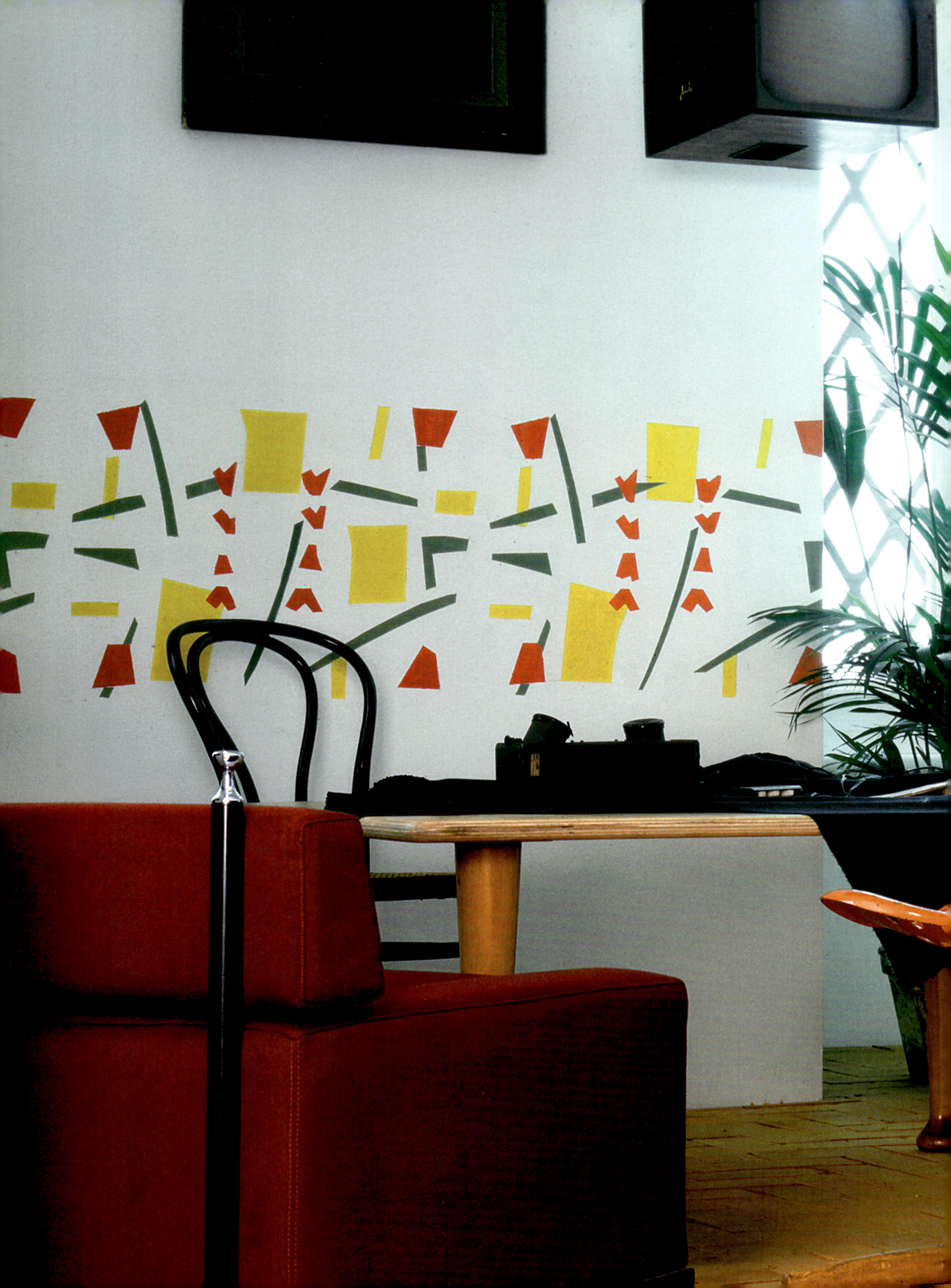

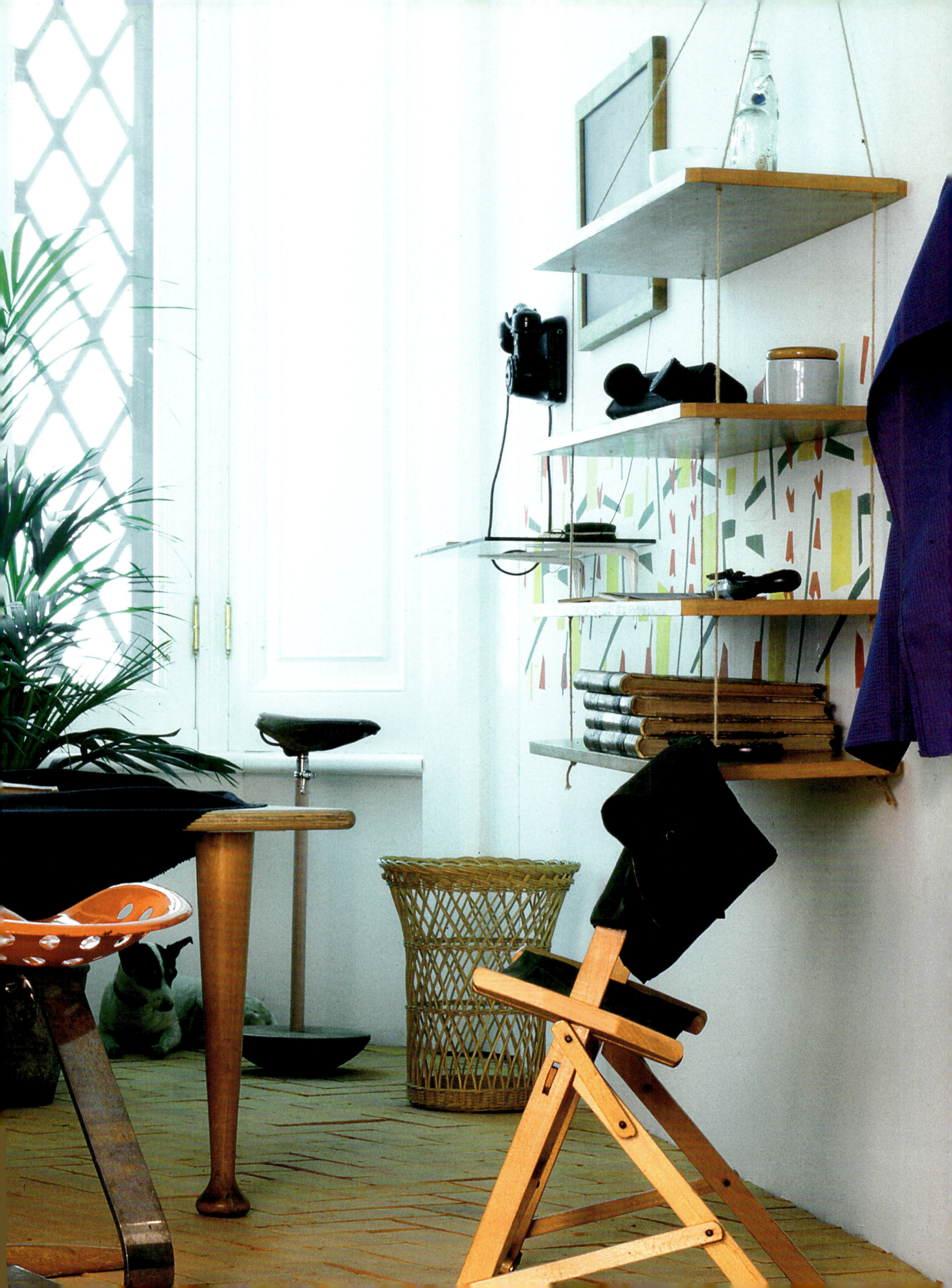

MEZZADRO

Designers: Achille and Pier Giacomo Castiglioni

Year: 1957

Company: Zanotta (1971)

Materials: stool comprised of a metal tractor seat, a stainless steel supporting leaf spring, and a solid beechwood cross bar at the base

It was Michele Provinciali who came up with the name of this famous stool by the Castiglioni brothers, Mezzadro. The reference to the agricultural world it implies (for the word means "sharecropper" in Italian) immediately suggests the idea of the domestic transposition of an object "stolen" from a tractor. This is one of the clearest examples of the designers' engagement with the method of readymades, reminiscent of Duchamp, whereby an everyday object is "moved" into an "inappropriate" environment in which it acquires unusual values, new figurative meanings, and a new expressive potential. An unripe version of the Mezzadro stool made its first appearance at the 10th Triennale in 1954, but it only entered into production seventeen years after its final version was presented in Villa Olmo in 1957. As a compositional collage, the object not only signalled the beginning of the "clever game" led by the Castiglioni brothers on the level of design, but also revealed the importance of gazing with curiosity and attention towards the world of material culture and its objects as an inexhaustible cultural-anthropological repository whose figures may be reassembled to form new combinations and in a Dadaist spirit brought into the domestic landscape. The Mezzadro is comprised of four elements: a tractor seat in stamped metal sheet, marked by round holes for transpiration; a curved leaf spring in stainless steel (it too originally from the tractor, but here turned upwards, so as to add flexibility to the seat); a wing screw (of the sort used for fastening bicycle wheels), which makes it possible to assemble the seat even without any utensils; and a solid beechwood foot, which joins the steel stem at a right angle, in such a way as to furnish the two additional points of support needed to lend stability to the stool.

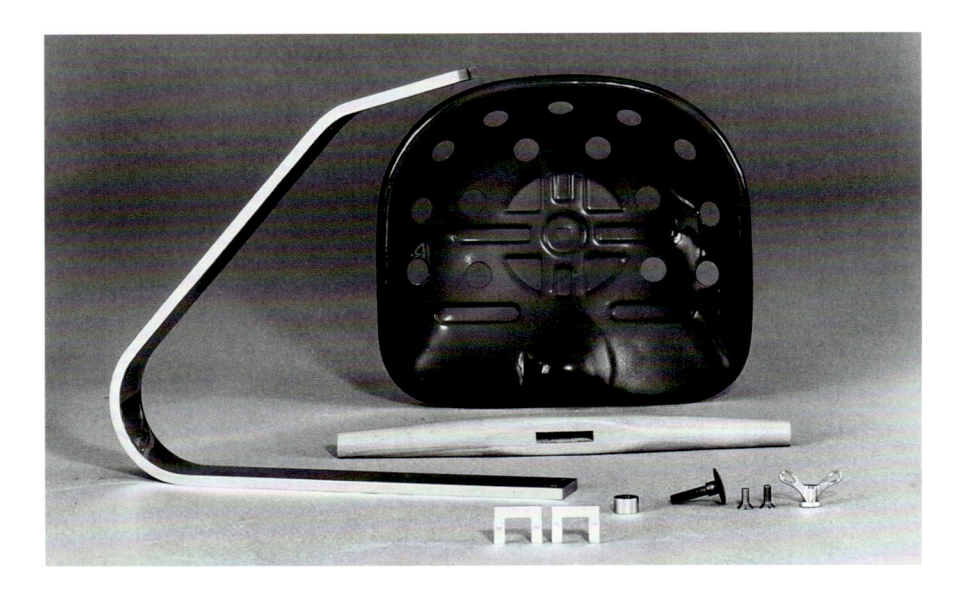

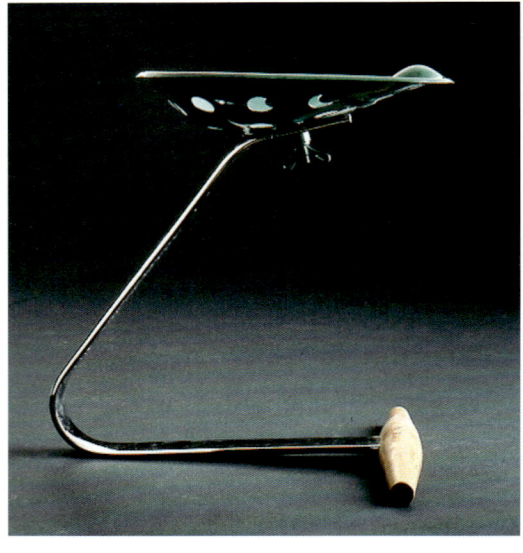

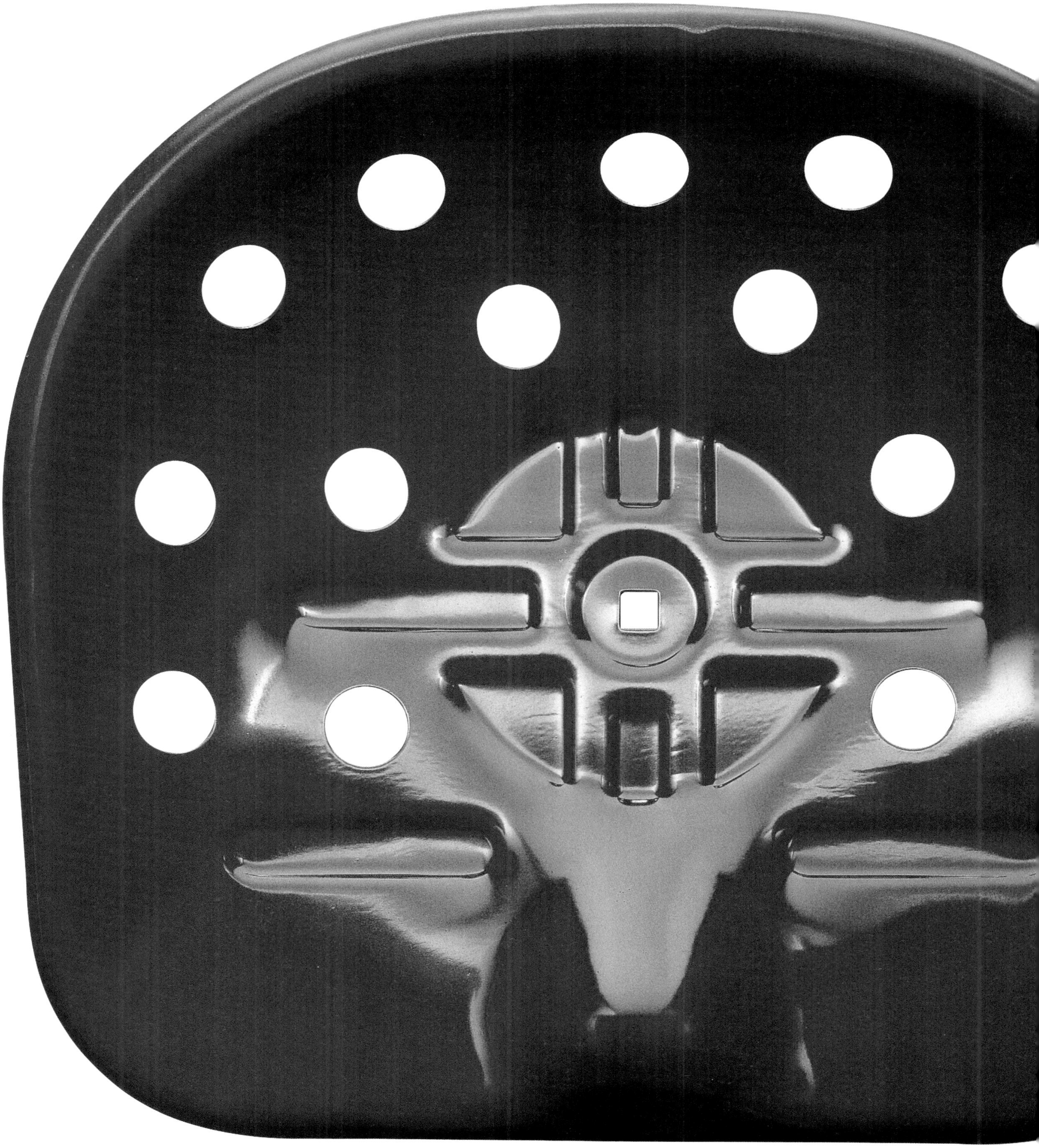

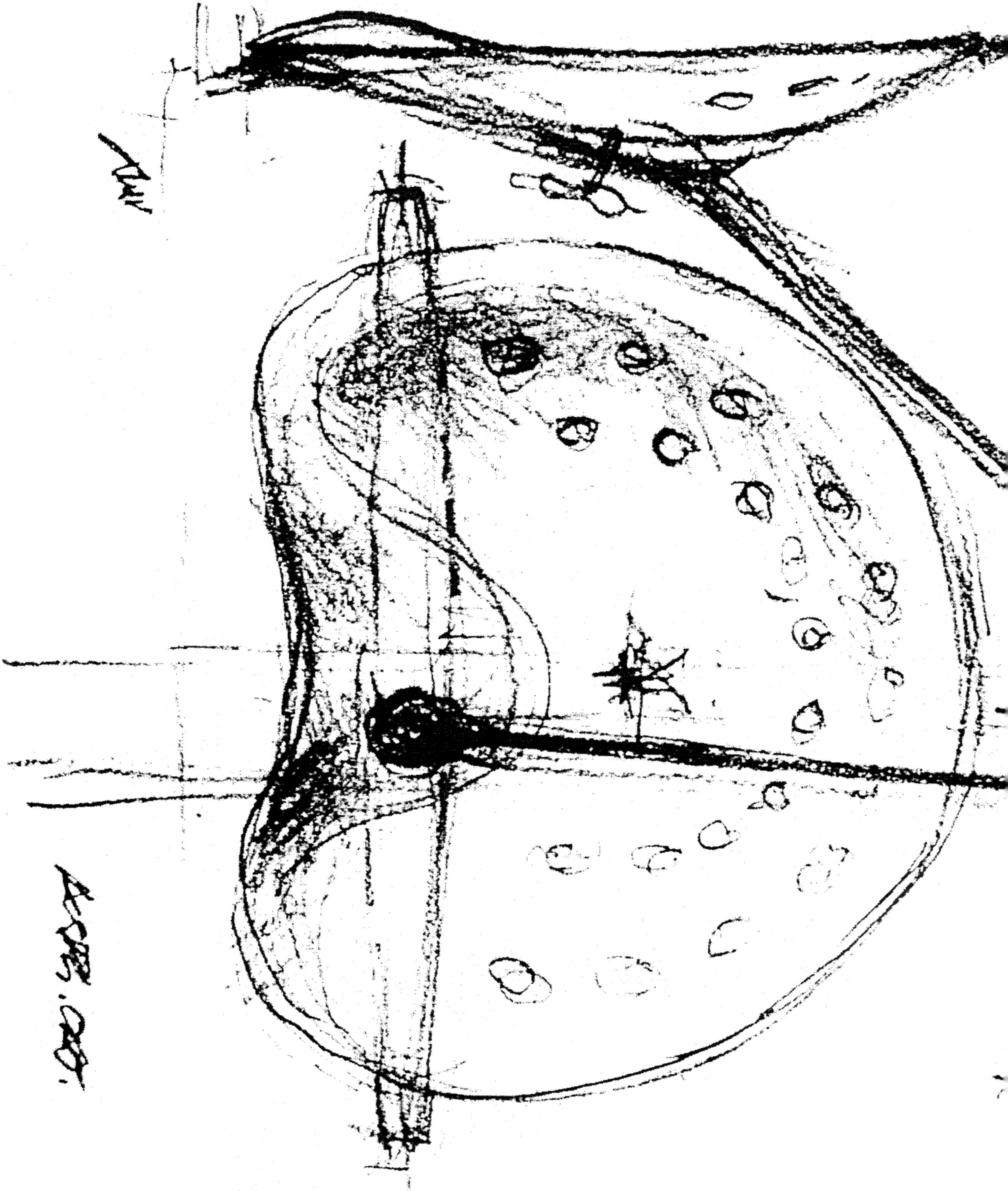

53

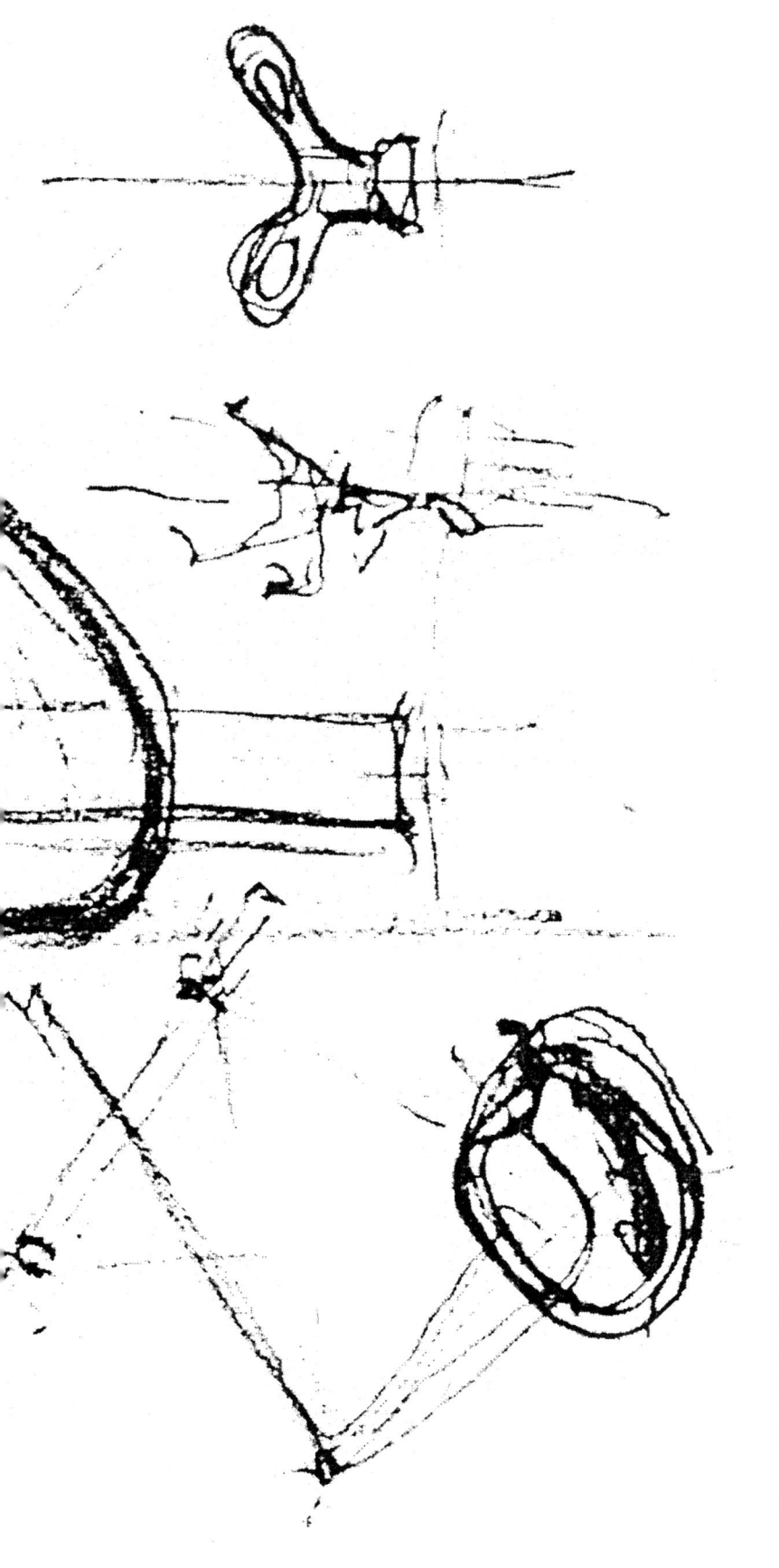

SELLA

Designers: Achille and Pier Giacomo Castiglioni
Year: 1957
Company: Zanotta (1983)
Materials: rocking stool, leather bicycle saddle, vertical metal tube fixed to a hemispherical cast-iron base

A *parent terribile* of Marcel Duchamp's famous *Roue de bicyclette* (1913), the Sella rocking stool was first presented on the occasion of the exhibition in Villa Olmo in Como (1957). Conceived as an answer to a specific behavioural and spatial requirement, this "corridor" seat sought to meet people's desire to speak over the phone without having to stand (since telephones in the 1950s were always on walls). Sella is part of the Castiglioni brothers' series of *objets trouvés*, items which through the readymade procedure would be assigned new utility functions in the domestic sphere. Sella entered into production thirty-four years later, to celebrate Francesco Moser's hour record. Despite its clear figurative reference to cycling, the object finds its typological matrix in the milking stool with a single central support. The wooden pivot of the original archetype is here replaced by a cast-iron hemisphere on which the pink vertical tube is fixed to support the saddle, whose height may be adjusted, as on a bicycle.

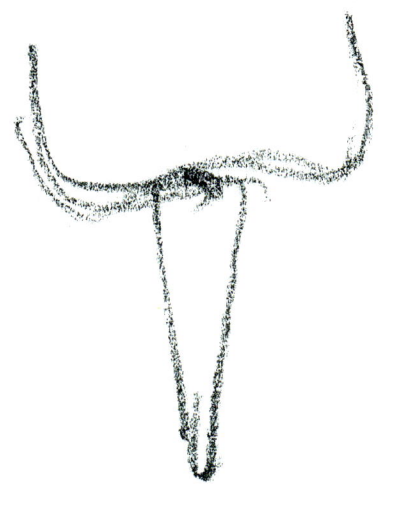

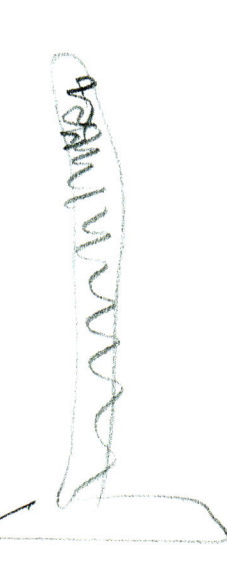

SEDILE TELEFONO

CHILDREN'S PHOTO-CAMERA

Designers: Achille and Pier Giacomo Castiglioni
Year: 1958 (prototype for Ferrania)
Material: shockproof plastic

This industrial design project foreshadowed the reference themes of contemporary design: low costs, practicality, and the object's high capacity to elicit emotions through its material and formal profile. Conceived for a public of newcomers to the world of photography, through its overall rounded profile the camera designed by the Castiglioni brothers for Ferrania embodies the idea of a "friendly" object, replacing the idea of high-tech with that of "high-touch": "this is not a photo-camera which 'feigns' luxury, as is often the case (with the use of faux leather, faux steel, faux exposure meters, faux graphic indexes, etc.), but rather a camera characterized and distinguished by a new and unique shape, which is only made possible by the use of plastic. And it attracts not through any "mimicry", but through imaginative allusions (to the world of science fiction). […] It was our belief that the unusual shape of the object would in itself be a good way to advertise it" (Achille and Pier Giacomo Castiglioni). The object combined a soft and enveloping shape, like that of polished stone, with ergonomic efficiency; and this, in age when photo-cameras were parallelepipeds with sharp corners. Forty years on, with the new models of global design in view, the camera's shape may regarded as an "archetype" of reference.

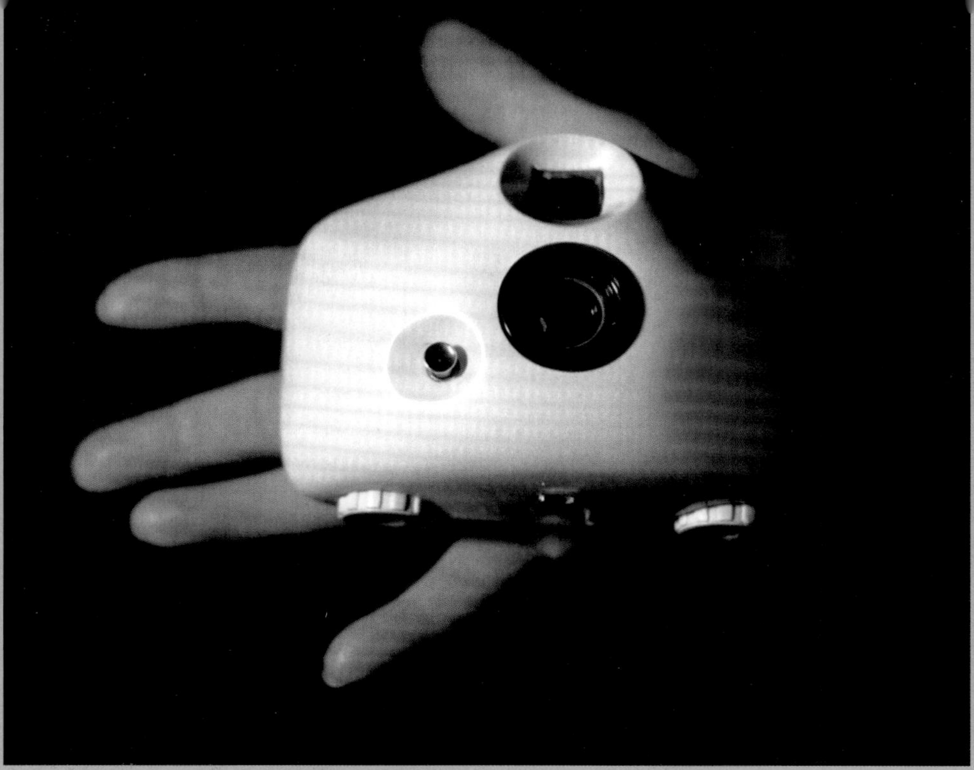

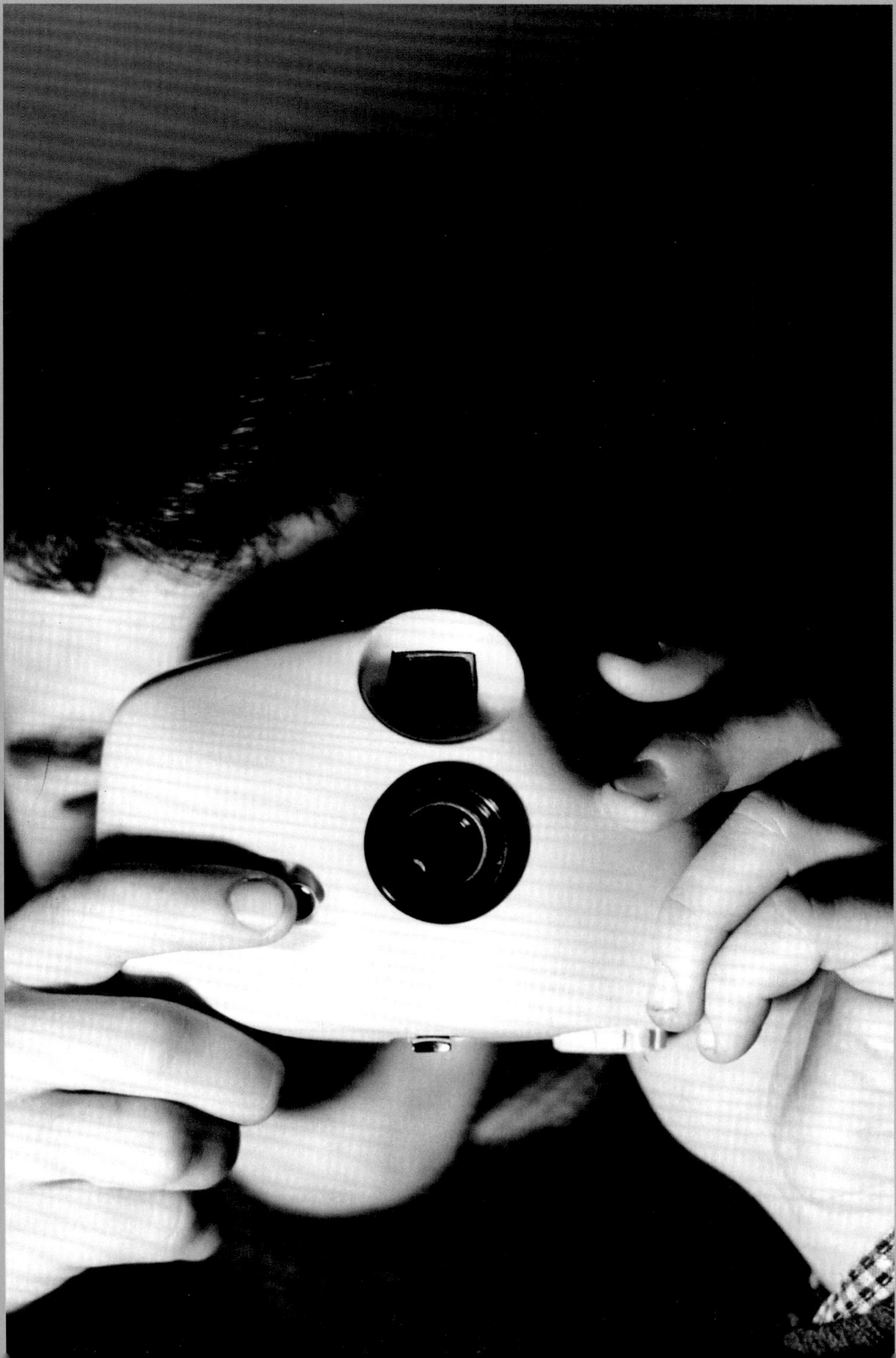

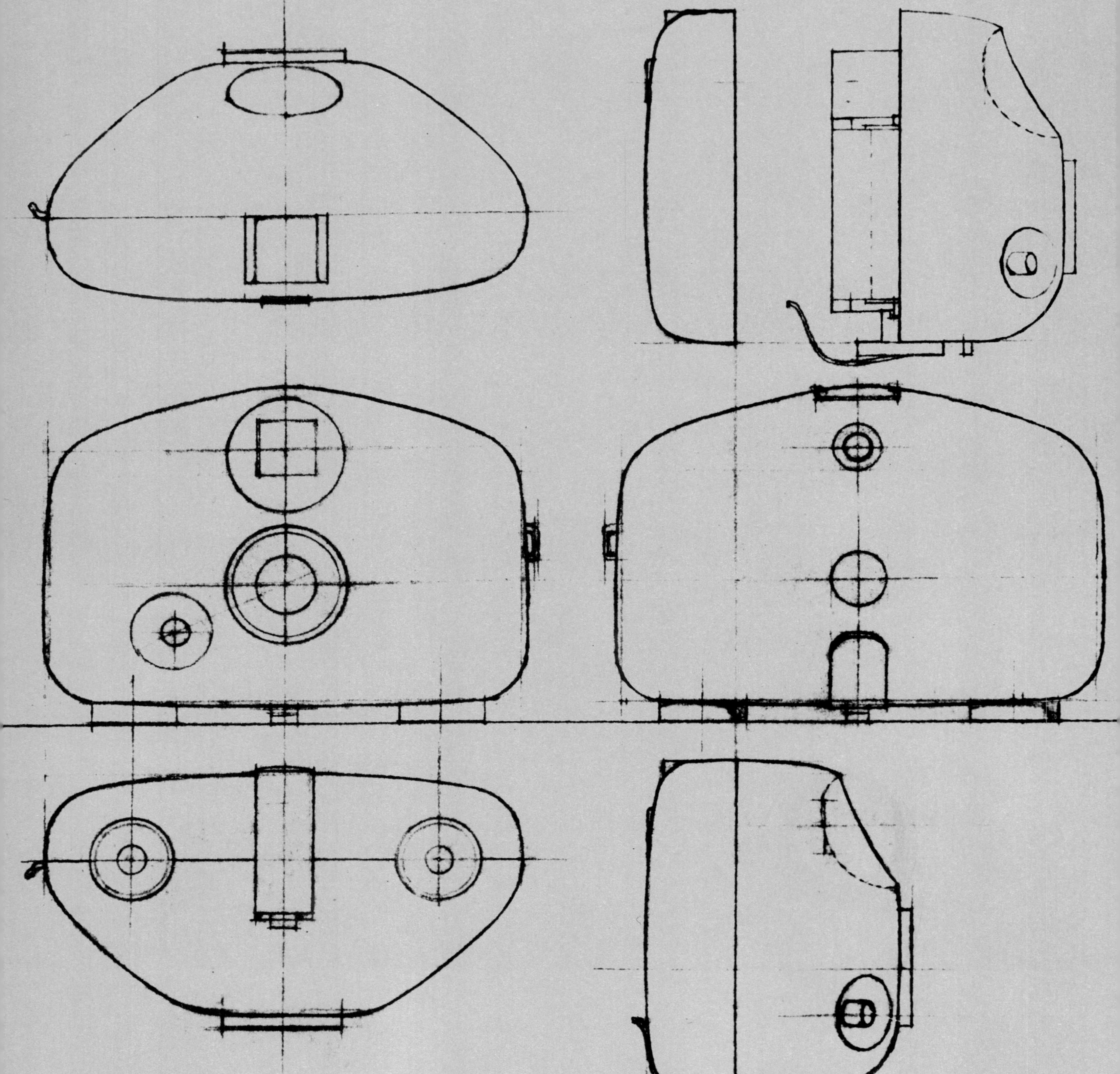

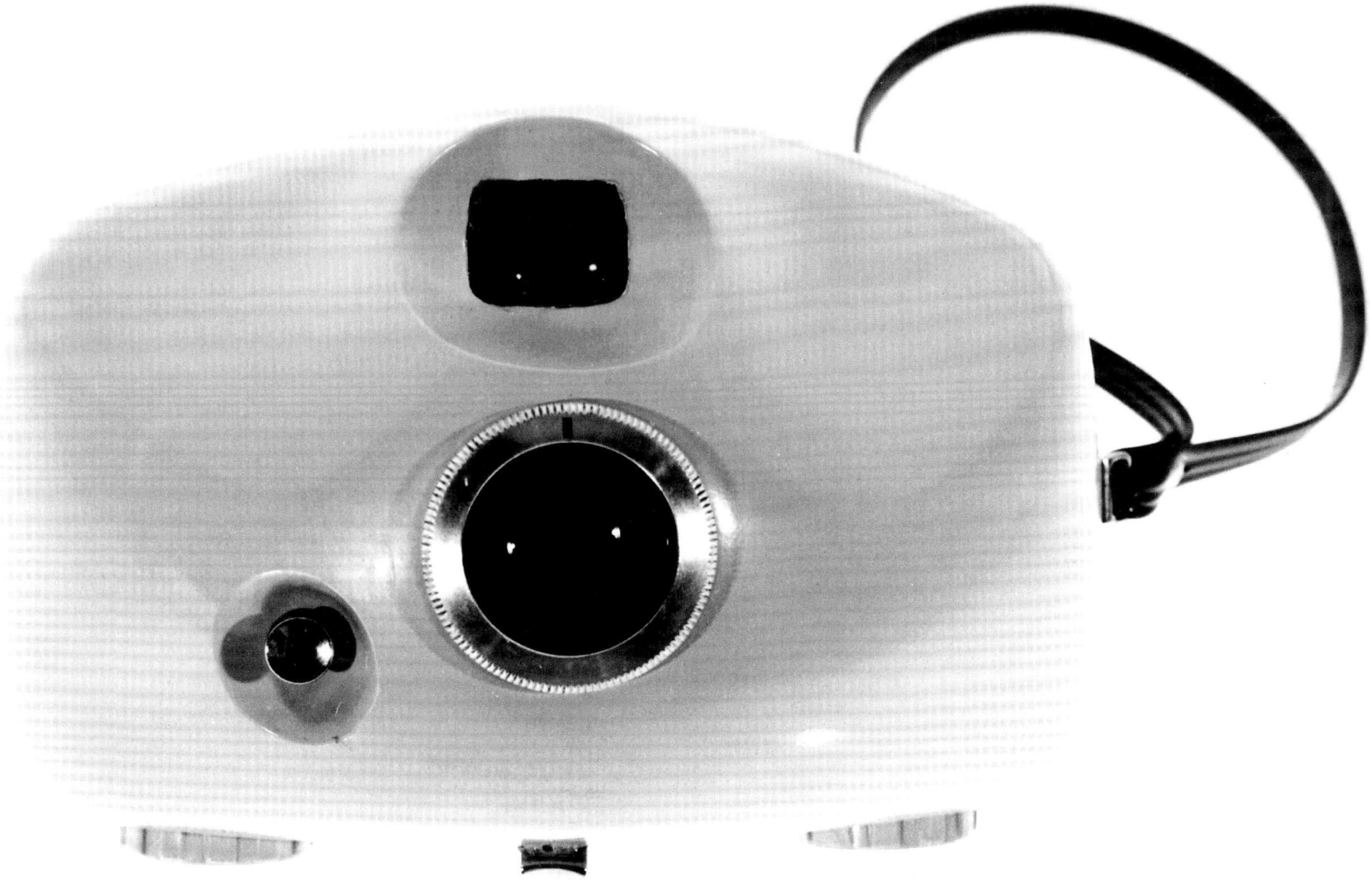

RAI PAVILION

Designers: Achille and Pier Giacomo Castiglioni
Years: 1957 (XXXV) and 1958 (XXXVI)

A small independent pavilion within the Milan Fair was devoted by the organizing body to the "Direzione Propaganda" department of the RAI. Between 1956 and 1963 (the year in which the small building was demolished), Achille and Pier Giacomo Castiglioni planned a series of exhibits geared towards a kind of experimental research in composition which foreshadowed highly topical themes such as the ideas of "building on the built" and of mixing architecture and communication technologies—in other words, the contemporary "media building".

As their guiding factors, the 1957 and 1958 editions had visibility from afar, the struggle to emerge as a landmark among the most imposing buildings of the Fair, the attempt to create a synergy between light and images, and the development of an effective semantic collage between the idea of pre-existing architecture and that of installation. Both solutions tended to vertically extend the limited size of the building, with its flat roof.

The 1957 project featured an aerial structure comprised of a metal system supporting a series of egg-shaped Flexa balloons with internal lighting; neatly arranged in four parallel rows and anchored through spherical sand counterweights, they were like Chinese lanterns transposed as effective figurative and luminous signs in the setting of the Fair. Within this structure RAI broadcastings were offered through sounds and spoken text recordings which could be listened to from five octagonal acoustic cabins. These defined the exhibit space while precluding any television images, in such a way as to stress the role of each viewer's imagination. The following year the exhibit took the form of a macro-sculpture connected to the theme of "broadcasting". The roof of the pavilion was turned into a small forest of coloured aerials. On the one hand, this provided a clever and effective communicative and expressive solution, stressing the linking of nations via Eurovision through bright lights and colours; on the other, it ironically played on the idea of the visual pollution of the city's roofs, which were becoming increasingly marked by the disorderly spread of private aerials.

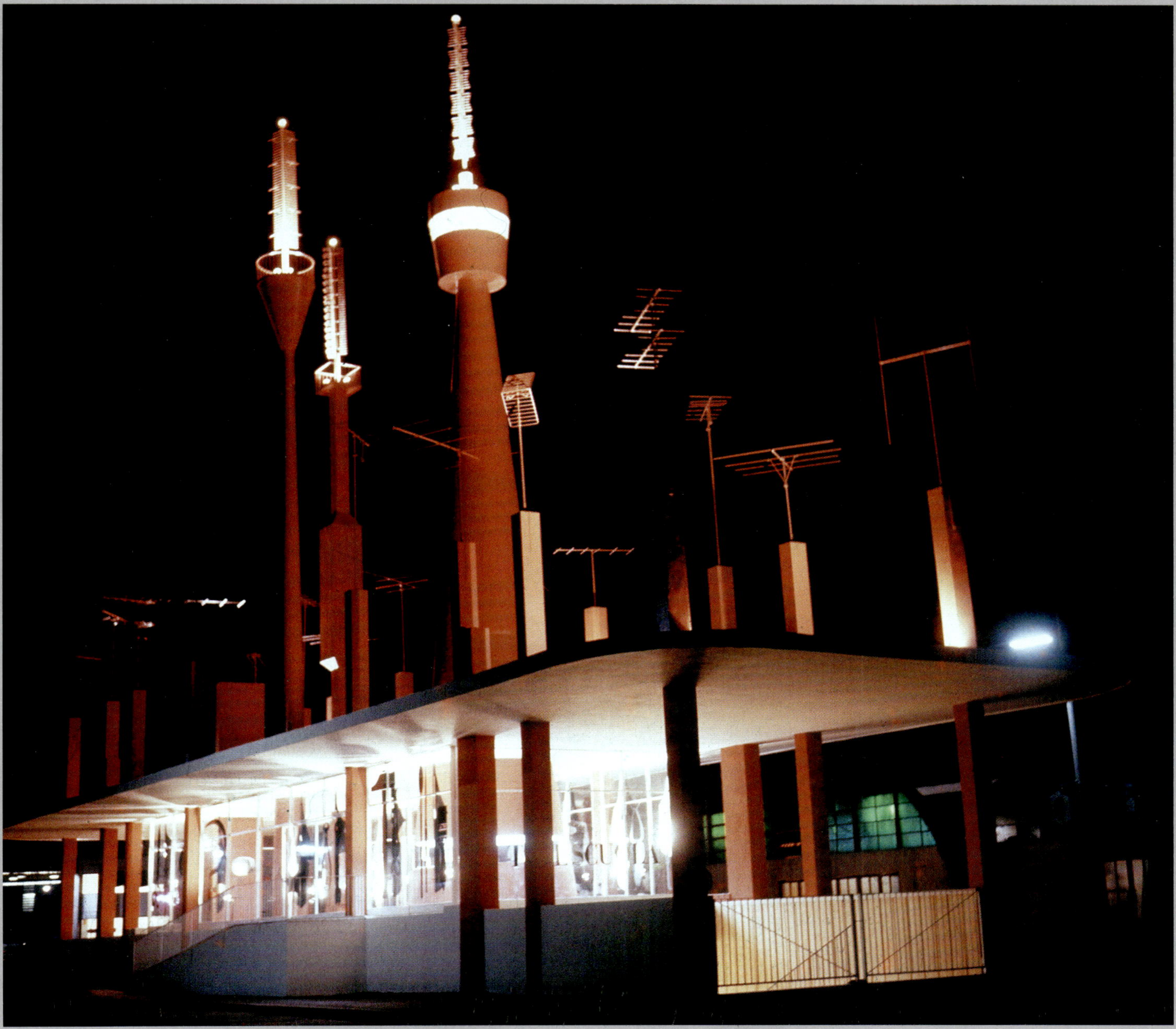

THE SPLÜGEN BRÄU BEERHOUSE AND RESTAURANT

Designers: Achille and Pier Giacomo Castiglioni
Graphic design: Max Huber
Year: 1960

This first example of a "designer restaurant" foreshadowed a phenomenon which has only really taken root over the last decade. To this day, the Splügen Bräu beerhouse and restaurant designed by the Castiglioni brothers in the centre of Milan in the early 1960s is a model for the interior architecture of public venues.
"We have designed the Splügen Bräu beerhouse as a very Milanese place. The Milanese are chatterboxes and like to be seen. So we have put them on display, as it were."
It was in these terms that Achille Castiglioni described the project for the first "designer restaurant" in the city, which was inaugurated in 1960 and demolished in 1981 to make space for a nondescript self-service restaurant. In their exemplary interior architecture project, the Castiglioni brothers combined a re-visitation of the Art Nouveau language, the creation of an area structured on various levels, and the modern aesthetics of ductwork in plain view. On the ceiling, the latter formed an intricate compositional web of bright brown enamelled pipes and ducts from which white trumpet-shaped loudspeakers hung, according to a careful arrangement, along with specifically manufactured or designed lighting devices. Among these was the famous Splügen Bräu suspended aluminium lamp, a classical item of Italian design that is still being manufactured by Flos almost half a century on.

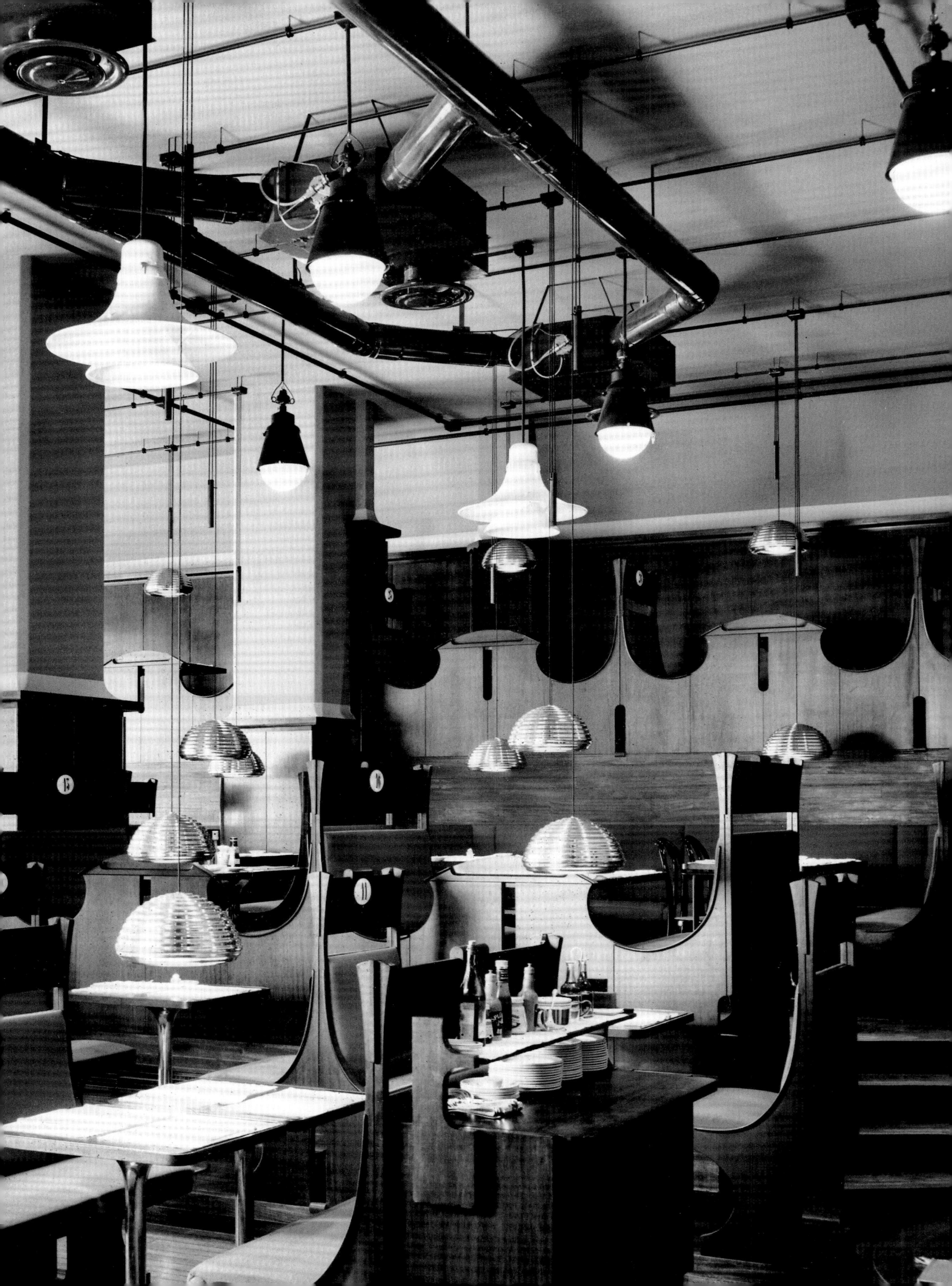

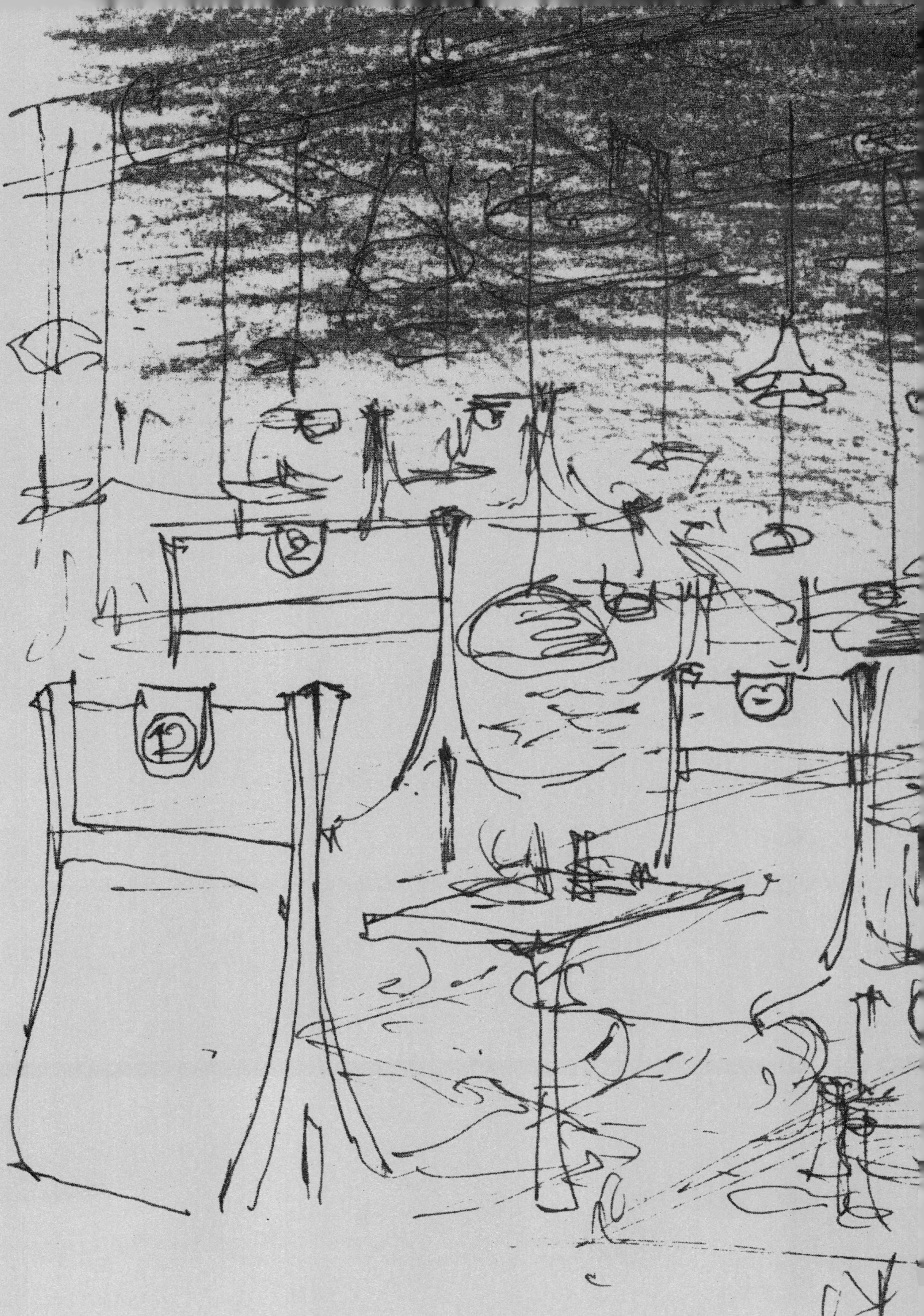

220/80

SPECHEN
BRAU

1962

SPLÜGEN BRÄU

Designers: Achille and Pier Giacomo Castiglioni

Year: 1960

Company: Flos (1962)

Materials: polished aluminium reflector, pulley made of a light die-cast alloy filled with lead shots

This suspension lamp was especially designed for the Splügen Bräu restaurant and beerhouse in Milan. One of the "classics" of Italian design, it is still being manufactured over forty years on. The project should be viewed in relation to the space in which it was meant to be installed: as a suspension lamp adjustable in height thanks to a counterweight attached to its power cable, it was capable of adapting to the various levels of the restaurant hall. The lamp was conceived in such a way as to shine light on diners' plates, not too far from the level of the table. So as not to disturb the diners' eyes, the reflector was made opaque, yet bright; its wavy surface ensures better heat loss. The air chamber inside the metal shell of the dome of the lamp prevents the silver-bowl bulb (then newly produced by Philips) from overheating. The bulb is totally concealed within the central section of the lamp.

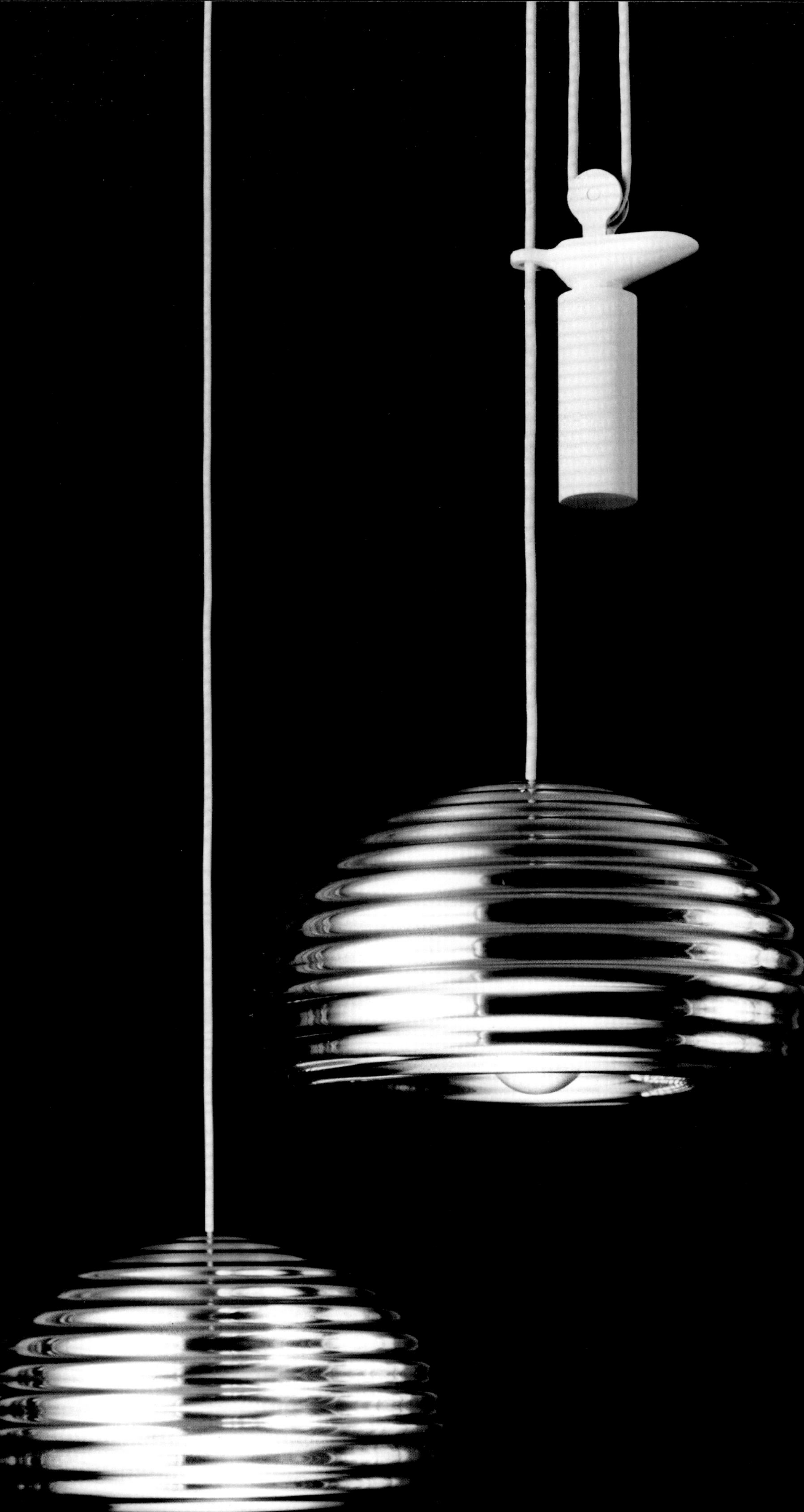

SERVI

Designers: Achille and Pier Giacomo Castiglioni
Year: 1961 (Servofumo, Servopluvio)
Designer: Achille Castiglioni
Years: 1974-1987 (Servomuto, Servomostre, Servostop, Servobar, Servolibro, Servomanto, Servobandiera, Servonotte, Servotutto, Servopedana)
Companies: Flos (1961), Zanotta (1974)
Materials: a system of service items, interior design objects in stove-enamelled steel with an ABS base

The first two items of this series, Servofumo and Servopluvio, were designed for the Splügen Bräu beerhouse and restaurant in Milan. However, they already possessed all the characteristics of objects belonging to a "system", in which equal components slide and mingle to serve different functions. The first two examples of what was destined to become a large family of service items over the course of twenty years—one further developed by Achille on his own—clearly revealed the constructive matrix of the series, consisting of a limited number of shared elements repeated to form different combinations. A black painted steel tube ending with an elegant knob for ease of handling supports a central steel bowl (serving as an ashtray). In the case of the Servopluvio, the latter is attached to the cone-shaped ABS base/ballast for collecting water from umbrellas. This model features a third constructive element, a curved, S-shaped rod, attached to the vertical tube in such a way as to support the umbrellas. The first two models signalled the beginning of a long series of products (Servobar, Servolibro, Servomanto, Servonotte, Servobandiera, etc.) developed by Achille Castiglioni. His Servomuto table (1976), a take on the English 18th-century "dumb-waiter" type, was probably the most interesting of these models: a striking example of "redesign", here used to create a "service table".

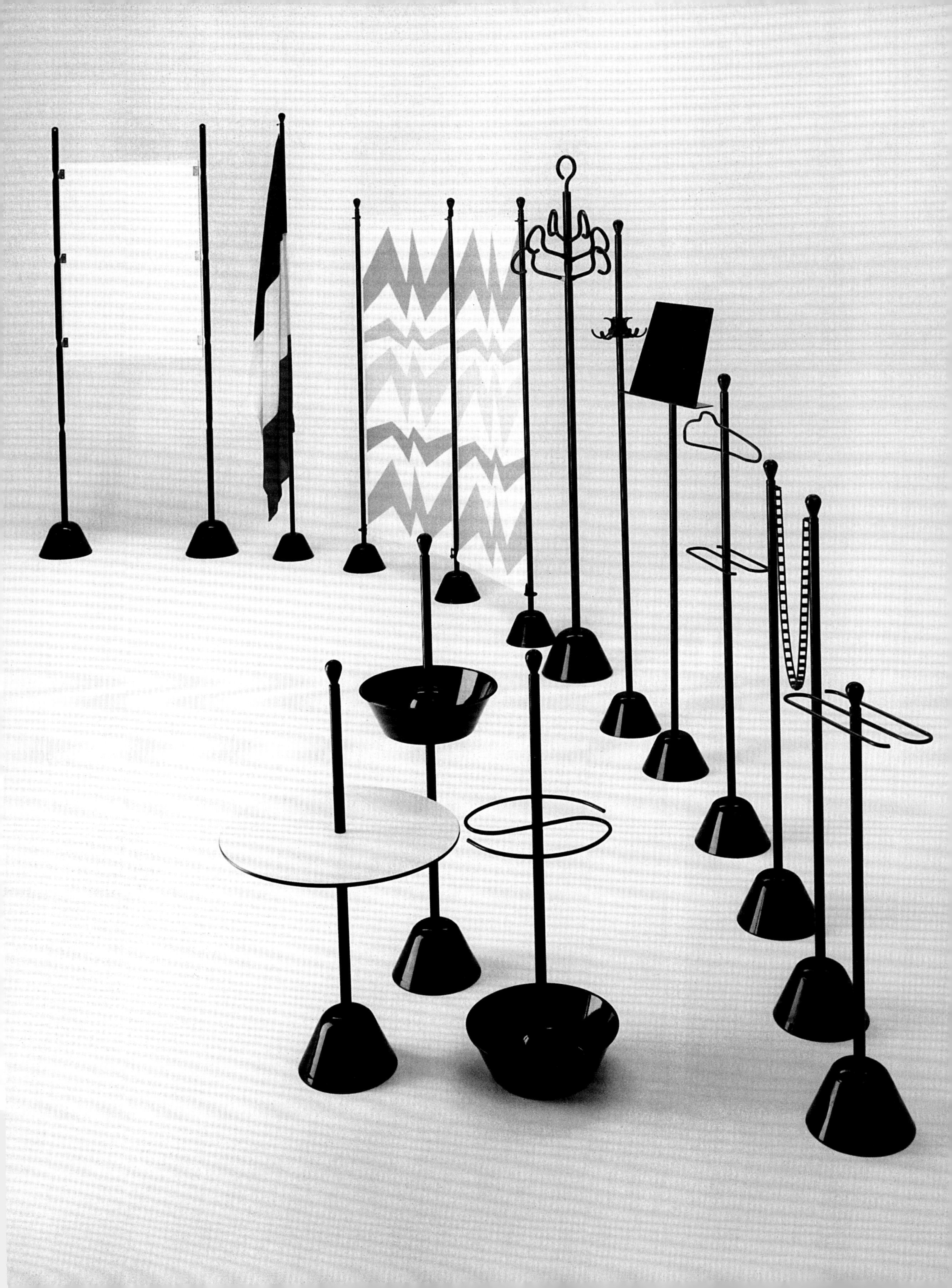

70

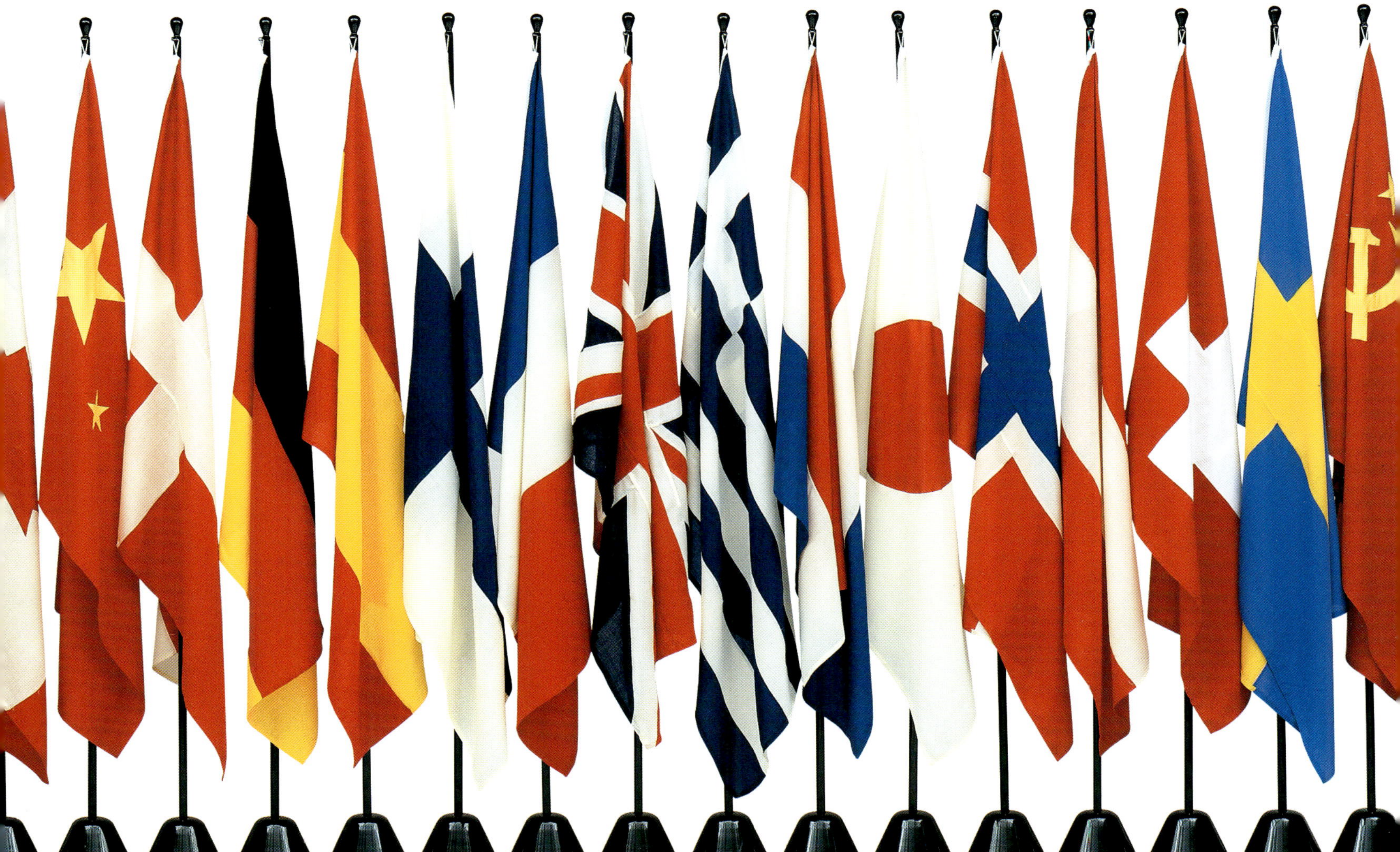

SANLUCA

Designers: Achille and Pier Giacomo Castiglioni
Year: 1960
Companies: Gavina, Knoll (1969), Bernini (1990), Poltrona Frau (2004)
Materials: seat and backrest with a metal supporting frame, padded with polyurethane foam and upholstered in cloth or leather, legs in lathe-turned rosewood

The Sanluca armchair is like the timeless symbol of a dynamic and innovative form of design. Almost reminiscent of Boccioni's sculpture, it anticipated serial assembly techniques in its components. It was a fixture ready for the assembly line of a furniture industry which had not yet reached maturity and was still developing. An exploded view drawing of the armchair reveals the rational approach of the project: the separate components of the object could be serially assembled, like those of cars. Other features the item has in common with the latter are the detailed ergonomic planning behind it and the idea of "speed" its outline conveys, as if it sought to express a dynamic shape as furniture: the winding Art Nouveau contour of the armchair gives it an aggressive and enticing profile, which transcends the concept of structural framing of the rationalist tradition, opening up new possibilities. This elegant plastic arrangement, however, was also intended to suit the "home of the Italians": a bourgeois house with period fittings and old pre-existing elements, rather than cold rationalist interiors. The Sanluca armchair was conceived in such a way as to stand out in any setting as a self-referential and self-contained piece, one destined—as its ongoing manufacture illustrates—to endure over time and become a "classic". Pier Giacomo Castiglioni told Dino Gavina: "[along with the Lierna (1960) chair, the Sanluca] seems an Art Nouveau piece: in this way, we can fool ladies who will buy a new piece thinking it is old." The armchair, which was designed in such a way as to perfectly adapt to all parts of one's body, consists of three separate components: a seat, a backrest, and a headrest. To these we must add the sides, ending with curved armrests. The supporting structure in pressed metal is padded with various layers of expanded polyurethane foam.

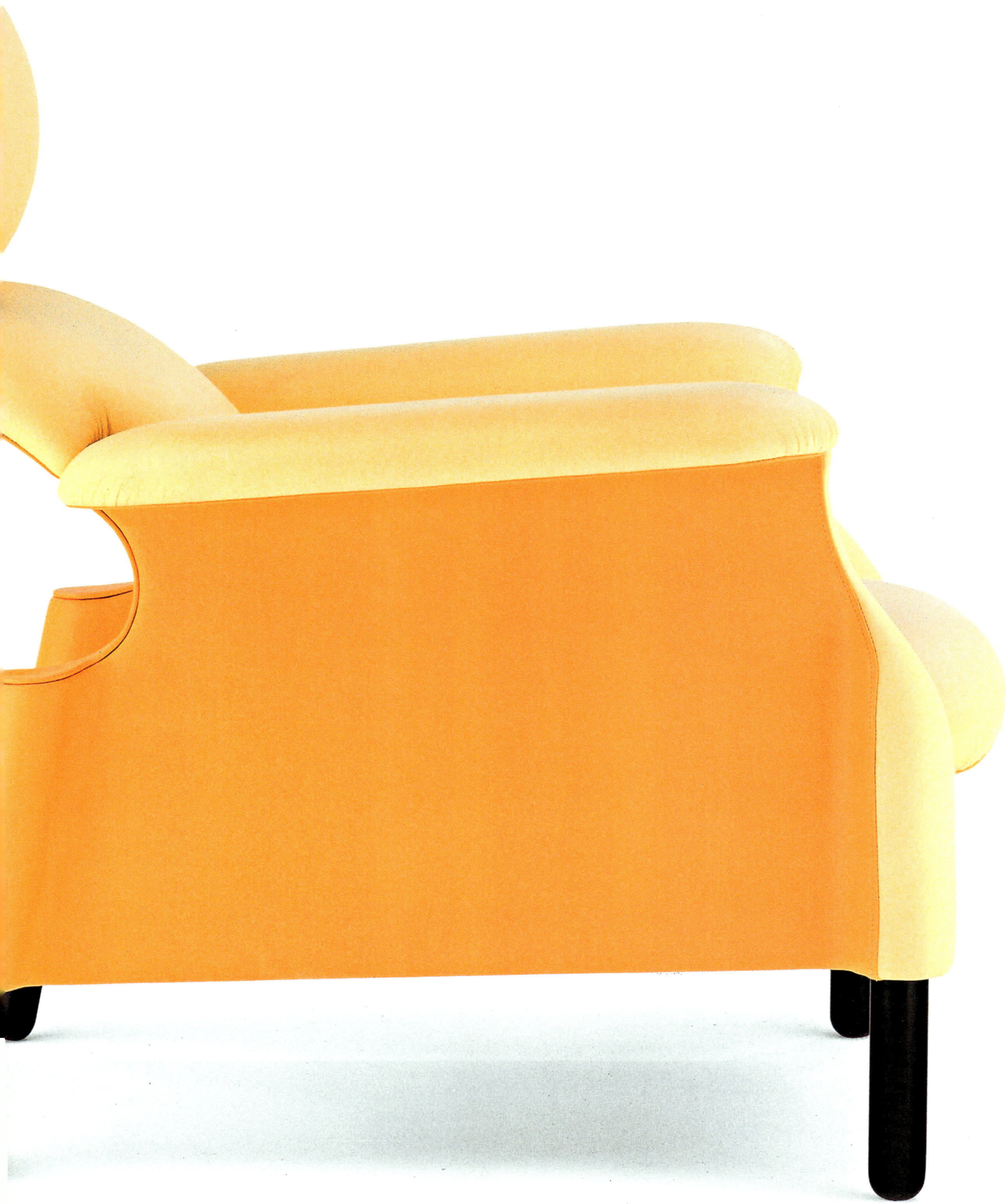

From left to right:
Michele Provinciali, Achille Castiglioni (kneeling),
Dino Gavina and Pier Giacomo Castiglioni

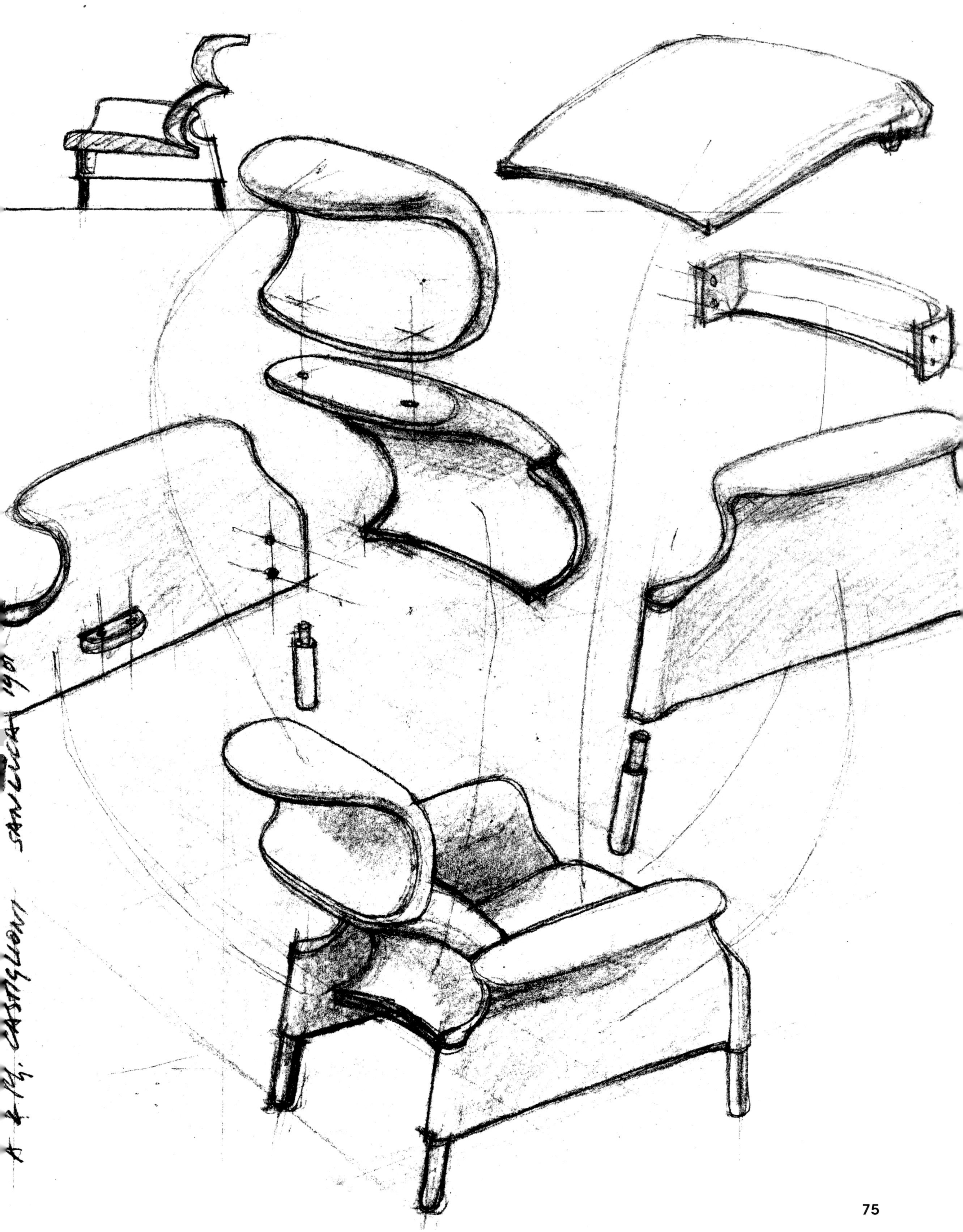
A & P.G. CASTIGLIONI SANLUCA 1961

TARAXACUM 60, VISCONTEA

Designers: Achille and Pier Giacomo Castiglioni

Years: 1960, 1962, 2005

Company: Flos

Materials: suspended lamps made from plastic polymers sprayed on a supporting metal mesh structure, patented by Heisenkeil

The Taraxacum 60 and Viscontea lamps illustrate the process of creation of a utility object through the reinvention and transposition of a material commonly employed for other purposes. In this case, the material used was a fibre, patented by the Heisenkeil company from Merano and made from sprayed plastic polymers, which solidified to form an elastic and resistant membrane. The Castiglioni brothers had seen this material applied to American military vehicles, in order to protect jeeps and tanks from the bad weather and salinity. While this technique had already been used in the field of design for some lamps designed by George Nelson and Isamu Noguchi in the early 1950s, the method developed by the Castiglioni brothers differed insofar as the sprayed film was only applied to the most protruding sections of the object and not to its entire perimeter. The inner structure of the lamps, consisting of a thin white metal rod, forms a light frame resembling unusual plant shapes (*taraxacum* is the Latin for dandelion). The film, stretched over the protruding portions of the inner frame, forms a single organic volume which looks not so much like a lighting device as a luminous and highly expressive sculpture. It is interesting to note that the creation of these models—which must have been extremely difficult to design, given the lack of computer graphics or 3D simulators in those days—is closely connected to experimental lab work of a kind not far removed from the artistic work of sculptors in their ateliers. The final effect, with various grades of "transparency" of the film, was achieved by spreading the polymers on the rotating structure, so that they would form a thick layer on the points of contact and a thinner one where the material is stretched.

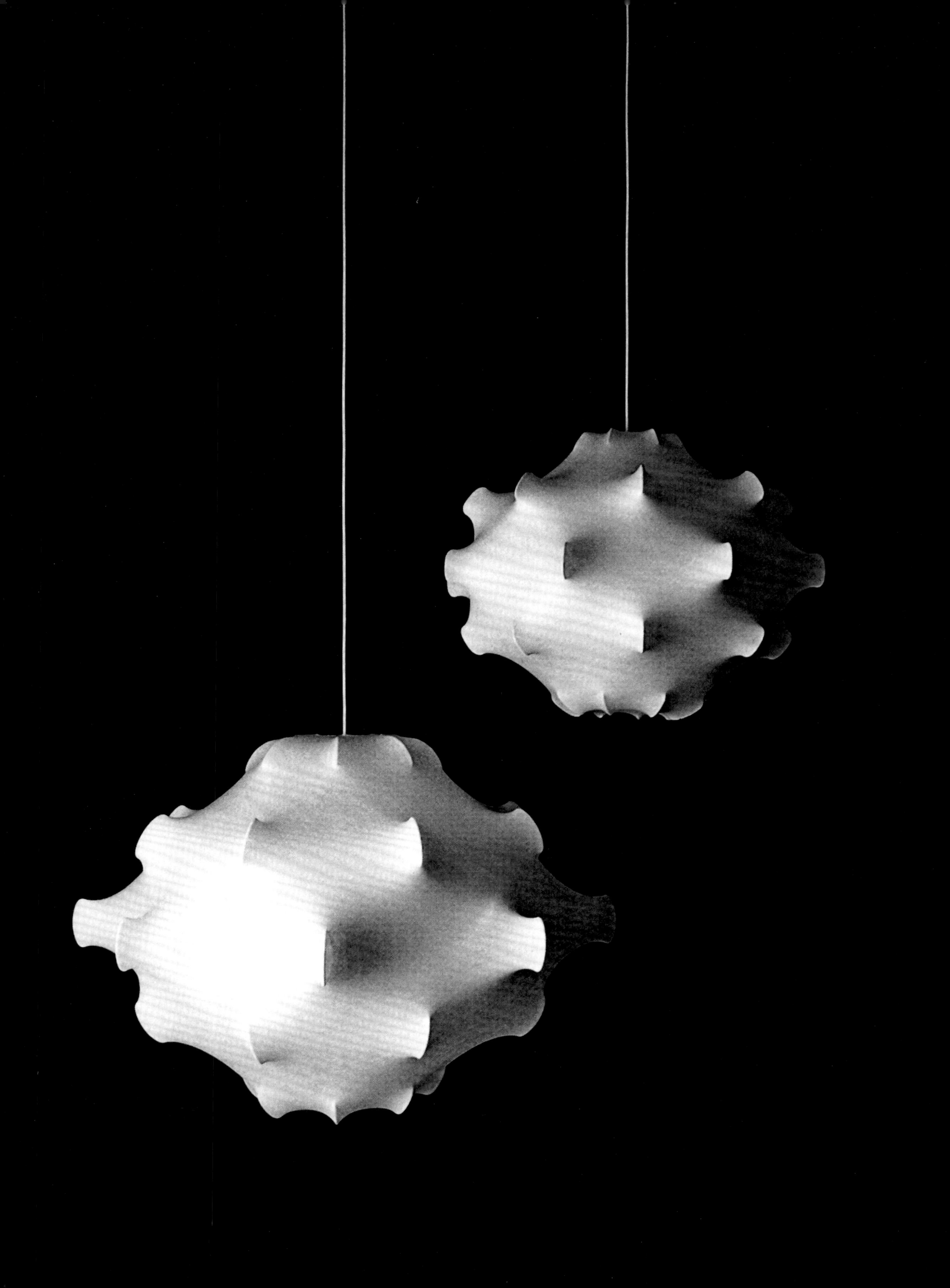

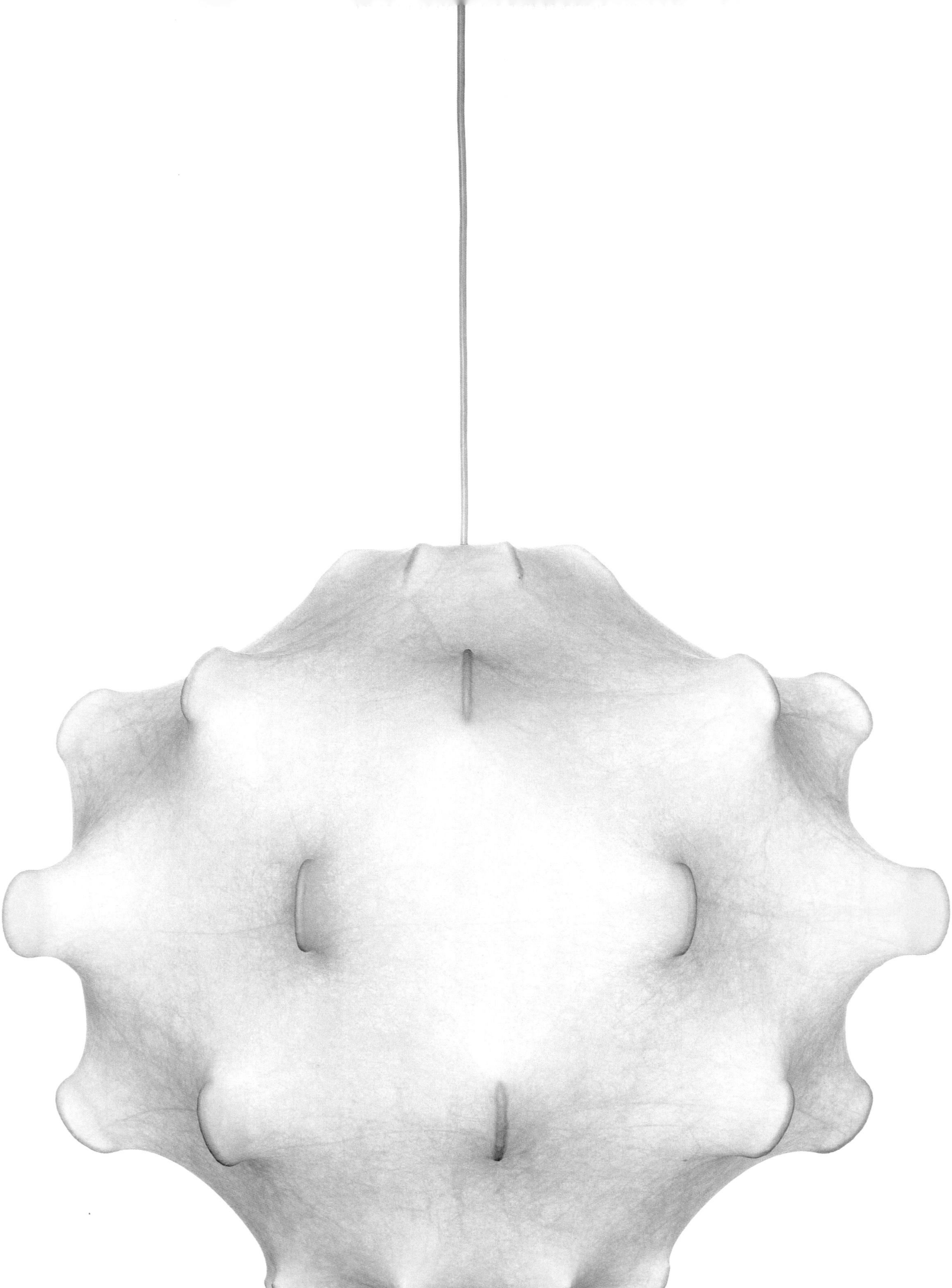

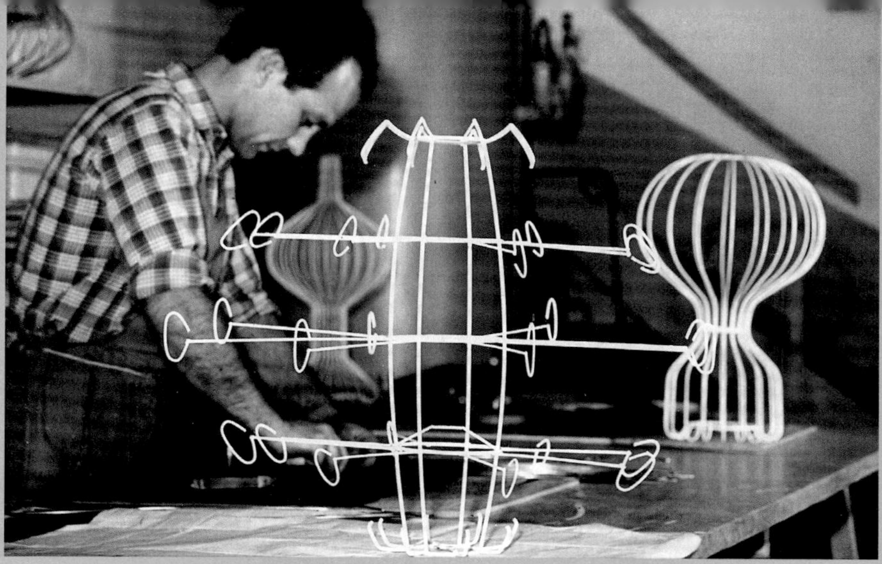

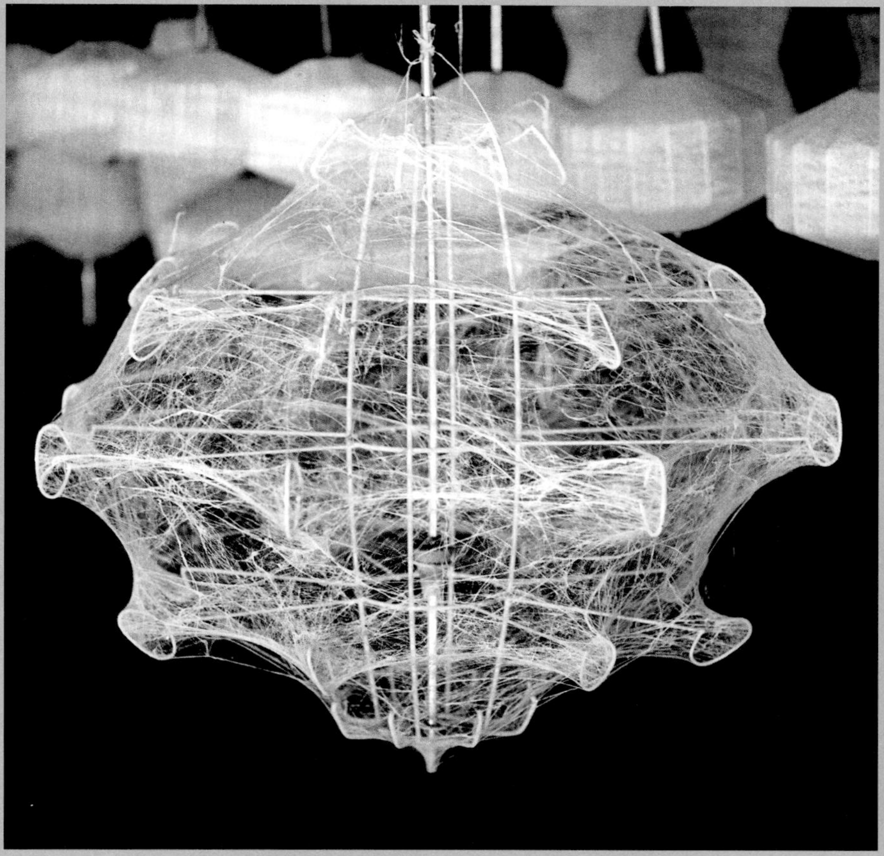

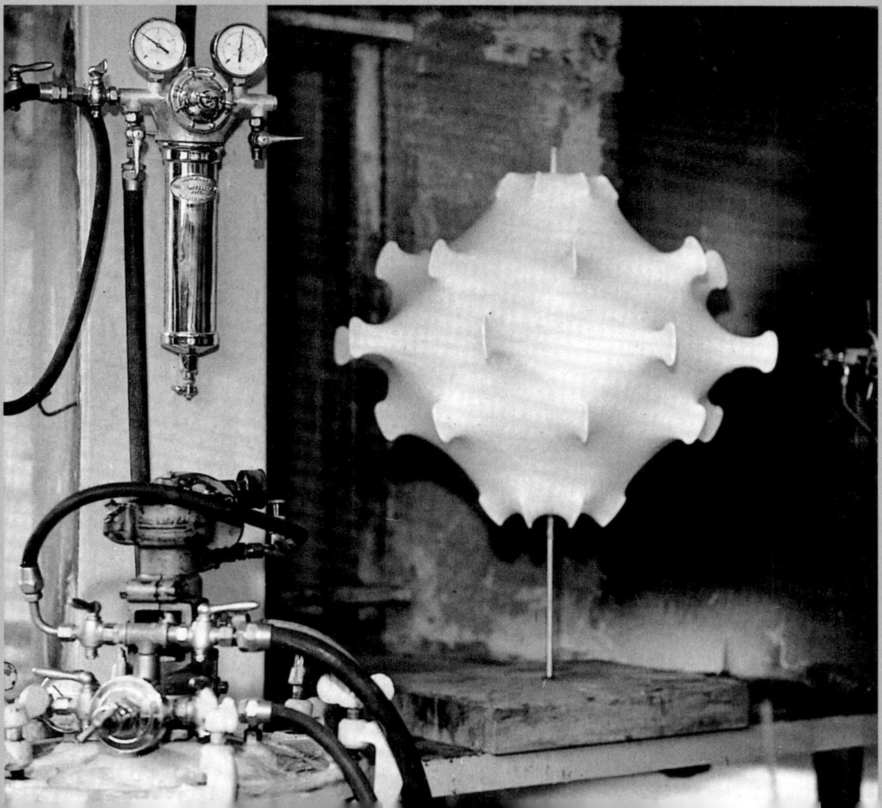

THE CASTIGLIONI STUDIO

Planners: Achille and Pier Giacomo Castiglioni

Year: 1961 (the Achille Castiglioni Studio from 1969; the Achille Castiglioni Studio Museum from 2006)

Poignantly described by Stefano Casciani as an "Ambrosian *Wunderkammer*", the studio of the Castiglioni brothers has remained intact for half a century, preserving its atmosphere as an incredible design workshop, "a magical space in which the most extraordinary marks of Italian design are concentrated, sedimented, stratified and displayed" (Dario Scodeller). The string of five rooms is filled with carefully numbered project folders of the same appearance, as well as collections of nondescript objects—tools of analysis and reflection for the development of new projects stored in glass medical cabinets. Fragments of items and a range of different objects unfold among the notes hung to the blind wall of the corridor. In the background, by the two rooms overlooking the Palazzo Sforzesco, a diagonally arranged mirror in the corner is transformed—from an element which meets a practical requirement (to see who walks in without having to move from the table)—into a metaphorical device: "it seems to be warning us that reality is precariously balanced and might capsize at any moment, and that this small vertigo is a discovery of oneself in relation to things and hence the beginning of a new embarking on invention and harmony" (Vittorio Gregotti). Through an agreement between Achille Castiglioni's heirs and the Milan Triennale, in 2006 the Castiglioni Studio was opened up to visitors as a testimony to Italian design and a heritage made available to a wider public.

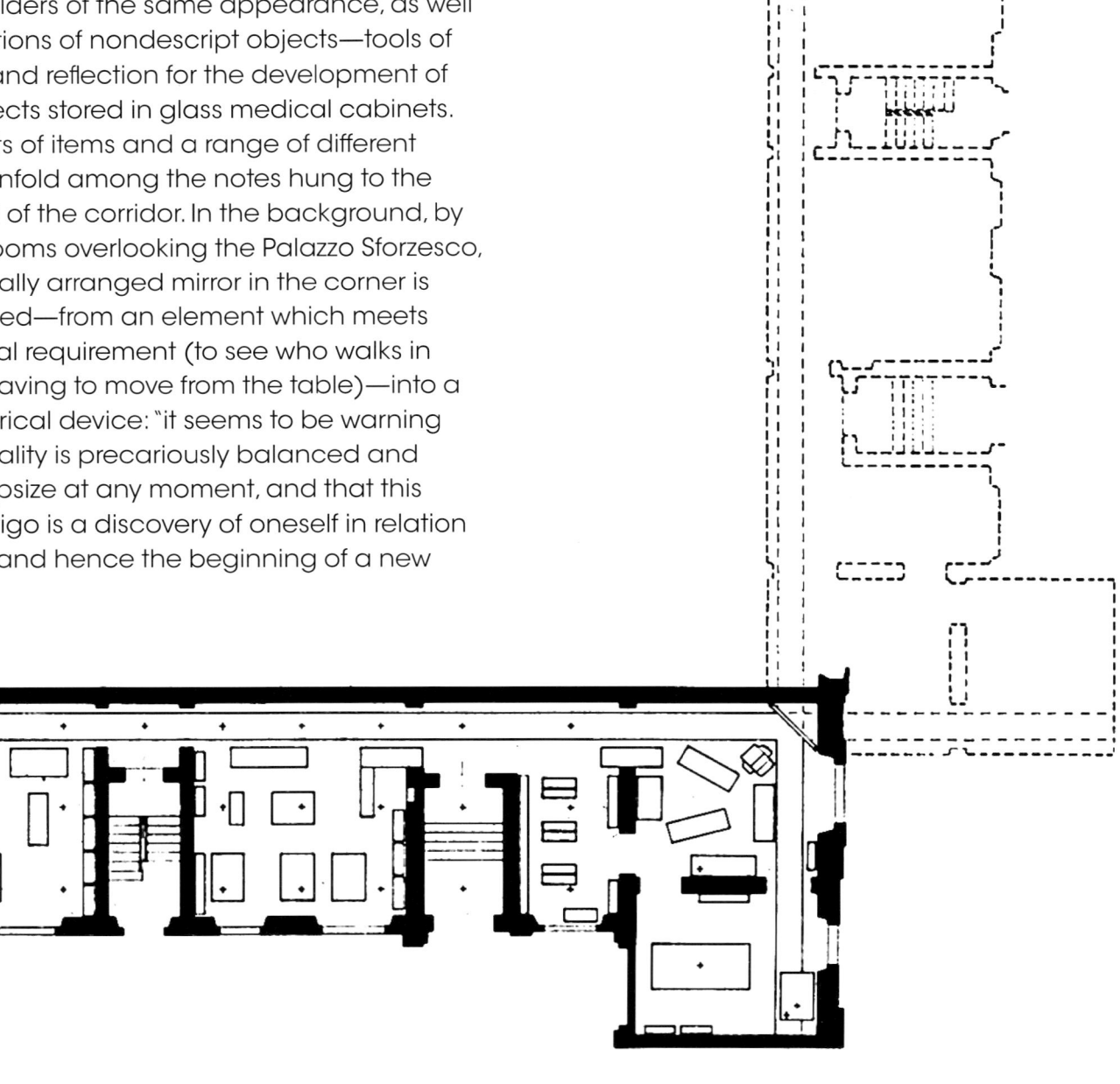

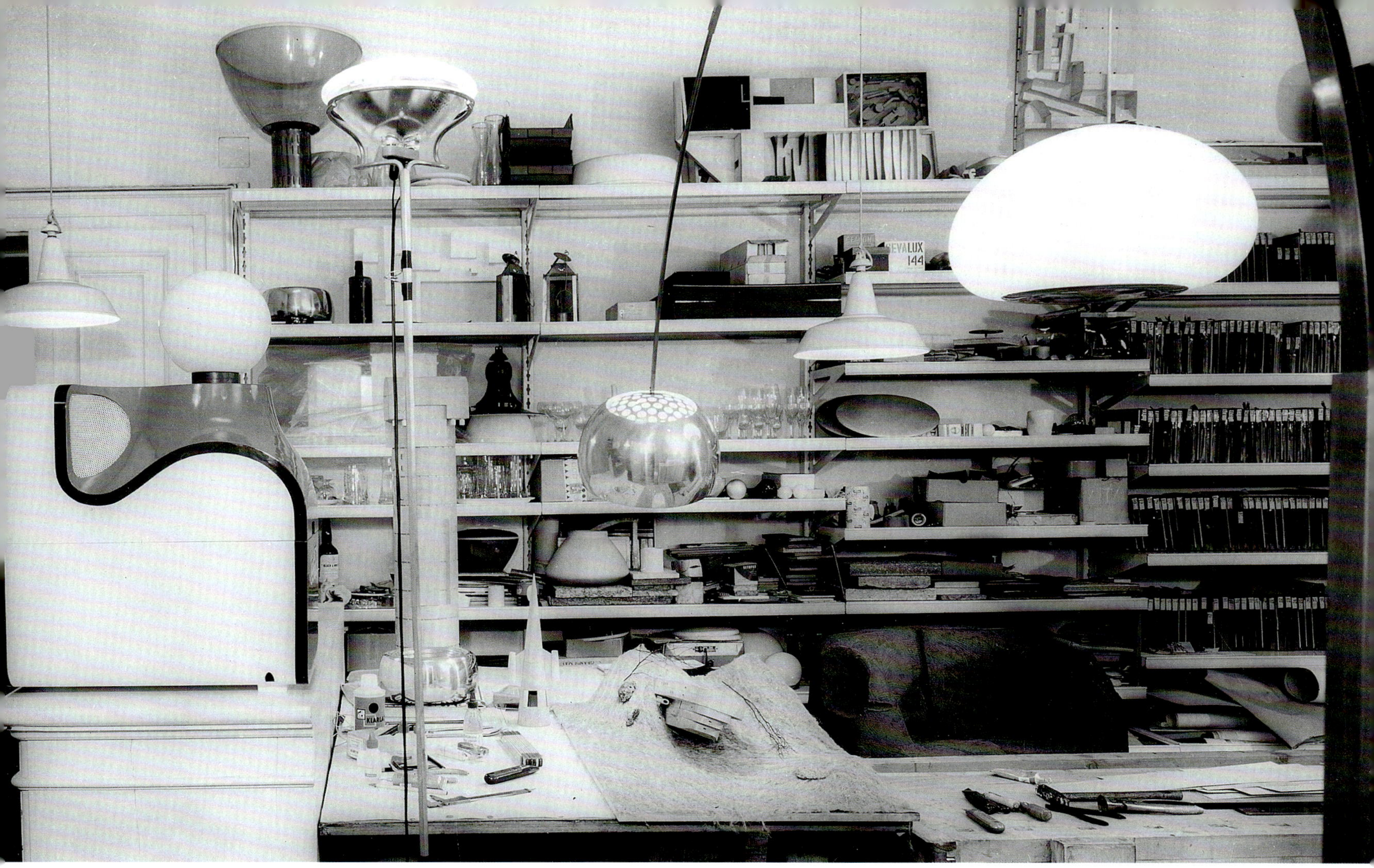
SEVALUX
144

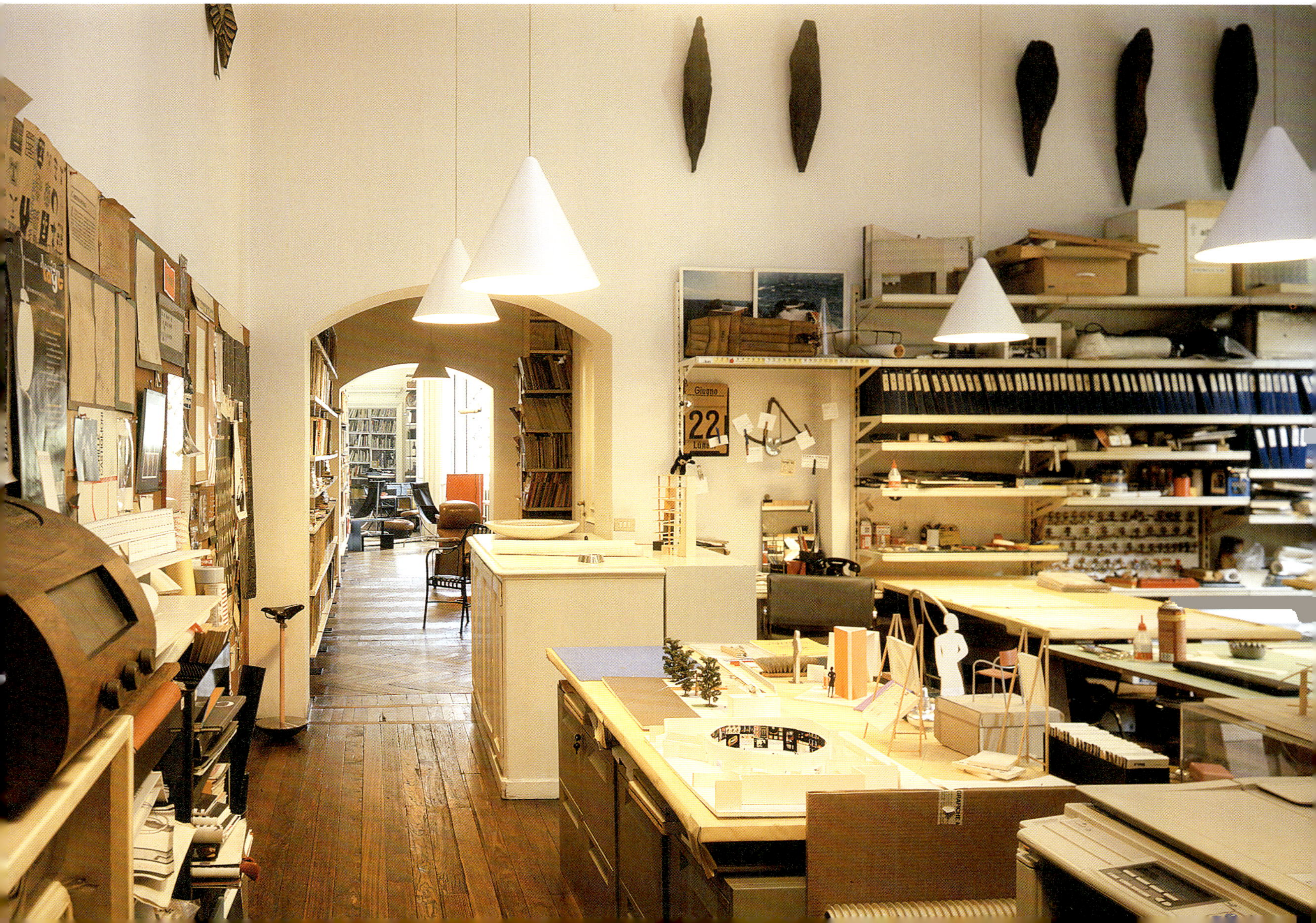
Giugno
22

TOIO

Designers: Achille and Pier Giacomo Castiglioni

Year: 1962

Company: Flos

Materials: adjustable height, car headlight with a silver crown, metal frame with a voltage transformer in plain view

The Toio lamp springs from the practice of creating readymades: from the collage-assemblage of *objets trouvés* whose mutual engagement and compositional combination gives rise to new items – in this case, an interior lamp. A 300-watt car headlight imported from the U.S. was inserted onto a spare metal supporting structure, which leaves the source of light in plain view. The electric wire passes through fishing-rod loops attached to a hexagonal metal stem. A voltage transformer, which serves as a counterweight to stabilize the lamp, is in plain view on the red enamelled metal base of the object, between two upside-down L-shaped profiles. Attached to these are both a supporting upright—with a wing screw for rewinding the wire— and a flat metal section curved at the top so as to join the one facing it, creating a sort of handle for carrying the device. Like the Luminator, this lamp, which is still in production, takes shape through the way in which its components are assembled.

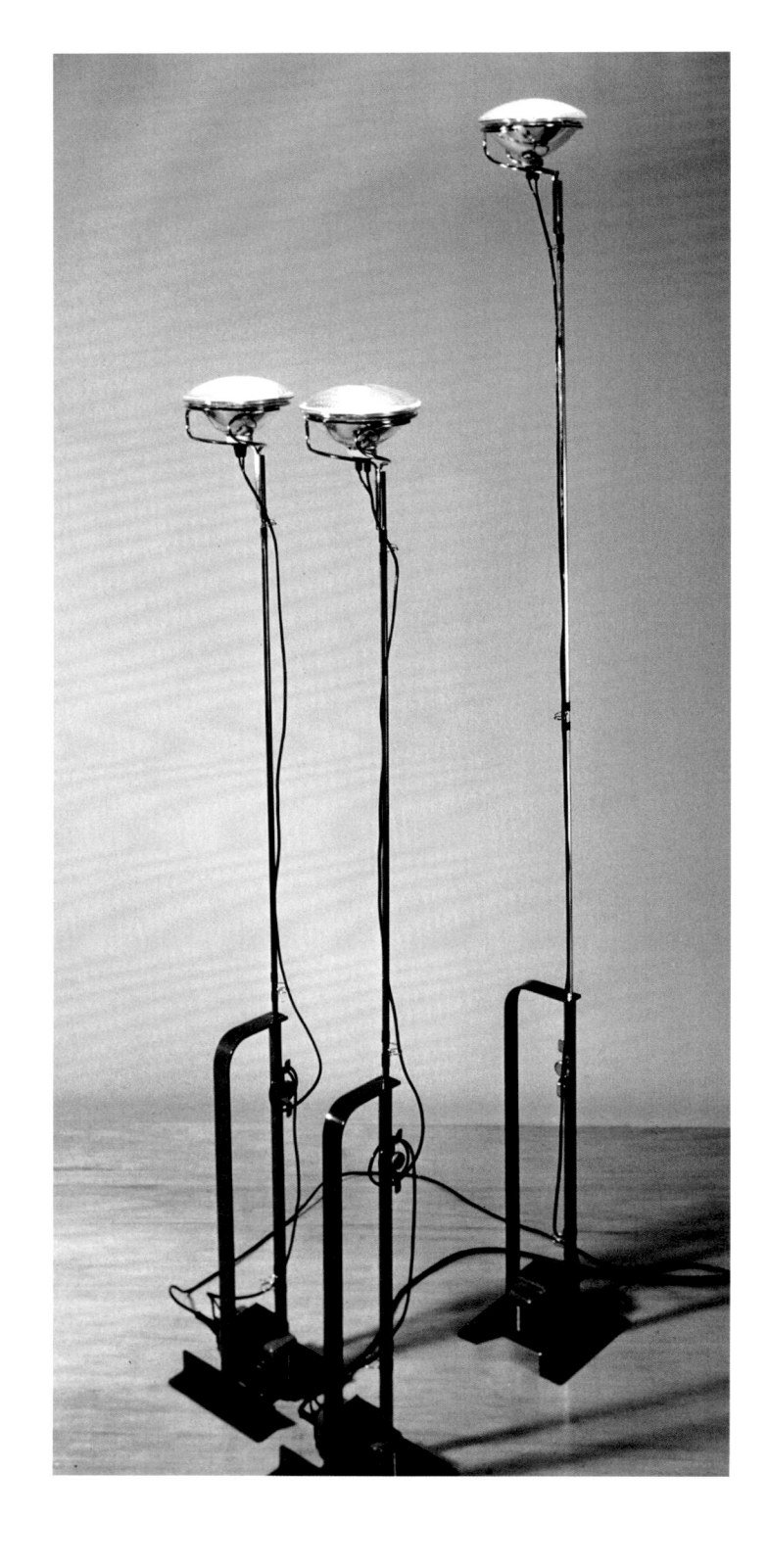

83

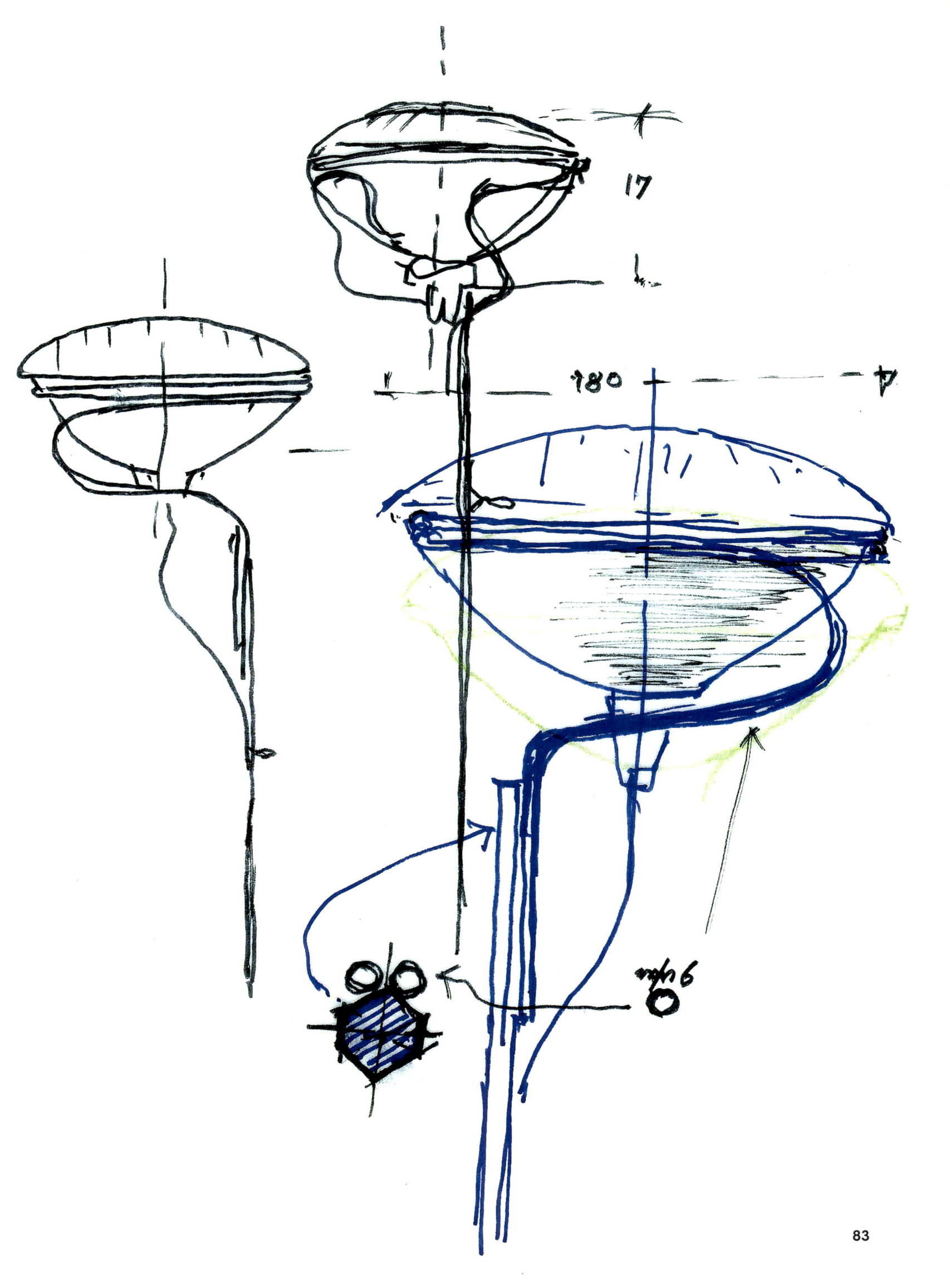

ARCO

Designers: Achille and Pier Giacomo Castiglioni
Year: 1962
Company: Flos
Materials: opal glass lamp socket, dome comprised of two superimposed elements in polished aluminium, telescopic stem comprised of three stainless steel elements, marble base

The idea behind the Arco lamp was to provide a kind of domestic version of a street lamp, enabling users to shine light from above in every corner of the house without having to worry about lighting points on the ceiling. The project first and foremost reflects a specific idea of space, or rather an idea of freedom in relation to the arrangement of the various rooms in a home based on the possibility of freely directing the light shining onto a table from above. "What we had in mind was a lamp which would shine on the table: there already were some, but you had to move behind them. In order to leave enough room around the table, the base of these lamps had to be at least two meters away. [...] The Arco has no decorative features: even the rounded edges at its base have a function, namely to avoid people colliding with them; even its hole is no mere whim: it's there to help us pick up the base" (Achille Castiglioni). The metal arc, consisting of a telescopic steel section, encloses the wiring. It is fixed to a marble parallelepiped with rounded edged which is marked by a circular hole, enabling users to anchor the object or move it, even through the insertion of a simple broomstick. The thin steel stem varies in thickness: it consists of three separate pieces which can telescope one into the other, enabling the light source to be set at an optimum distance. The angle of the light may also be adjusted thanks to the superimposition of two polished aluminium domes, one of which is perforated to facilitate cooling and to diffuse a little light towards the ceiling.

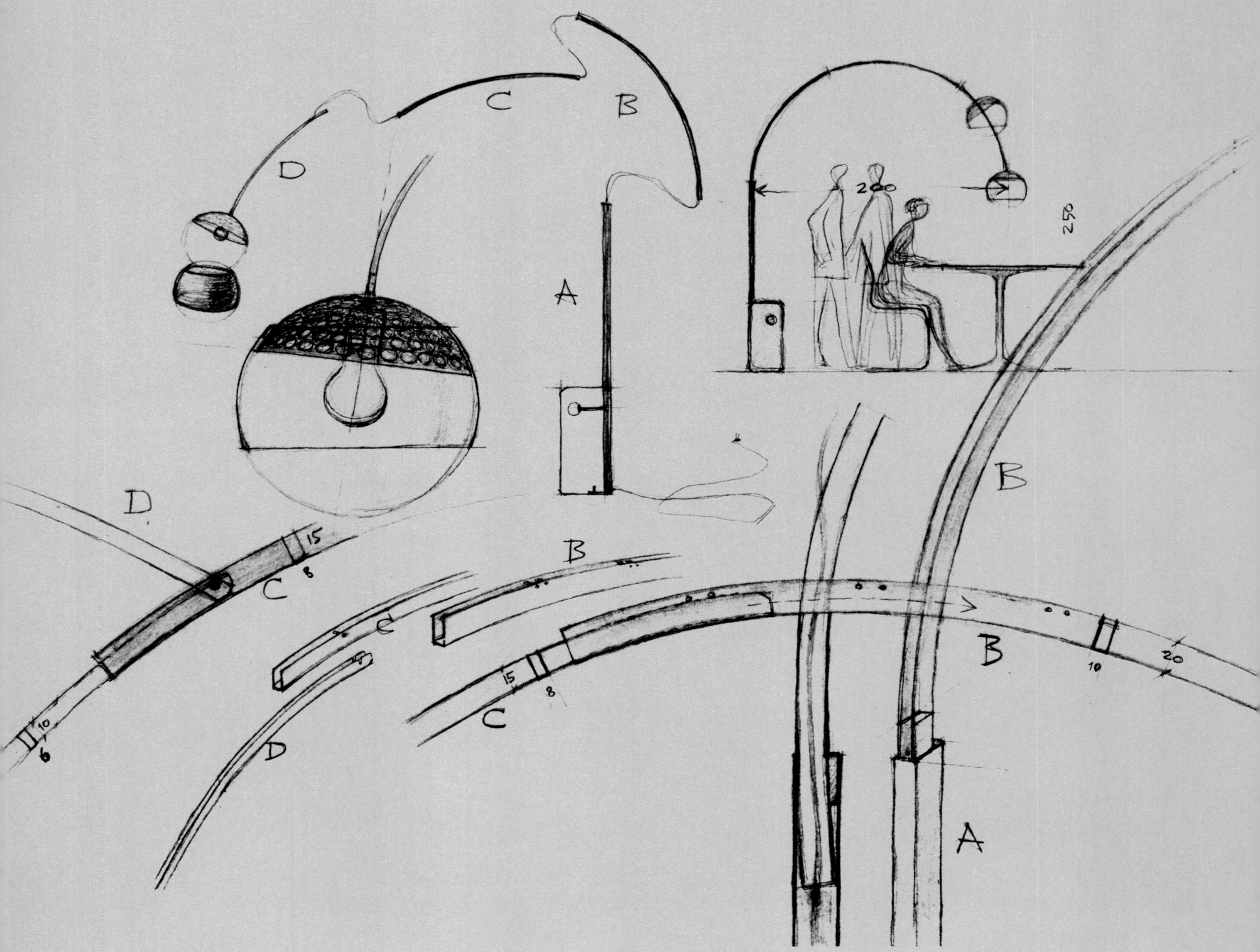

C
B
D
A
200
250
D.
15
8
C
B
C
10
6
D
B
15
8
C
B
10
20
A

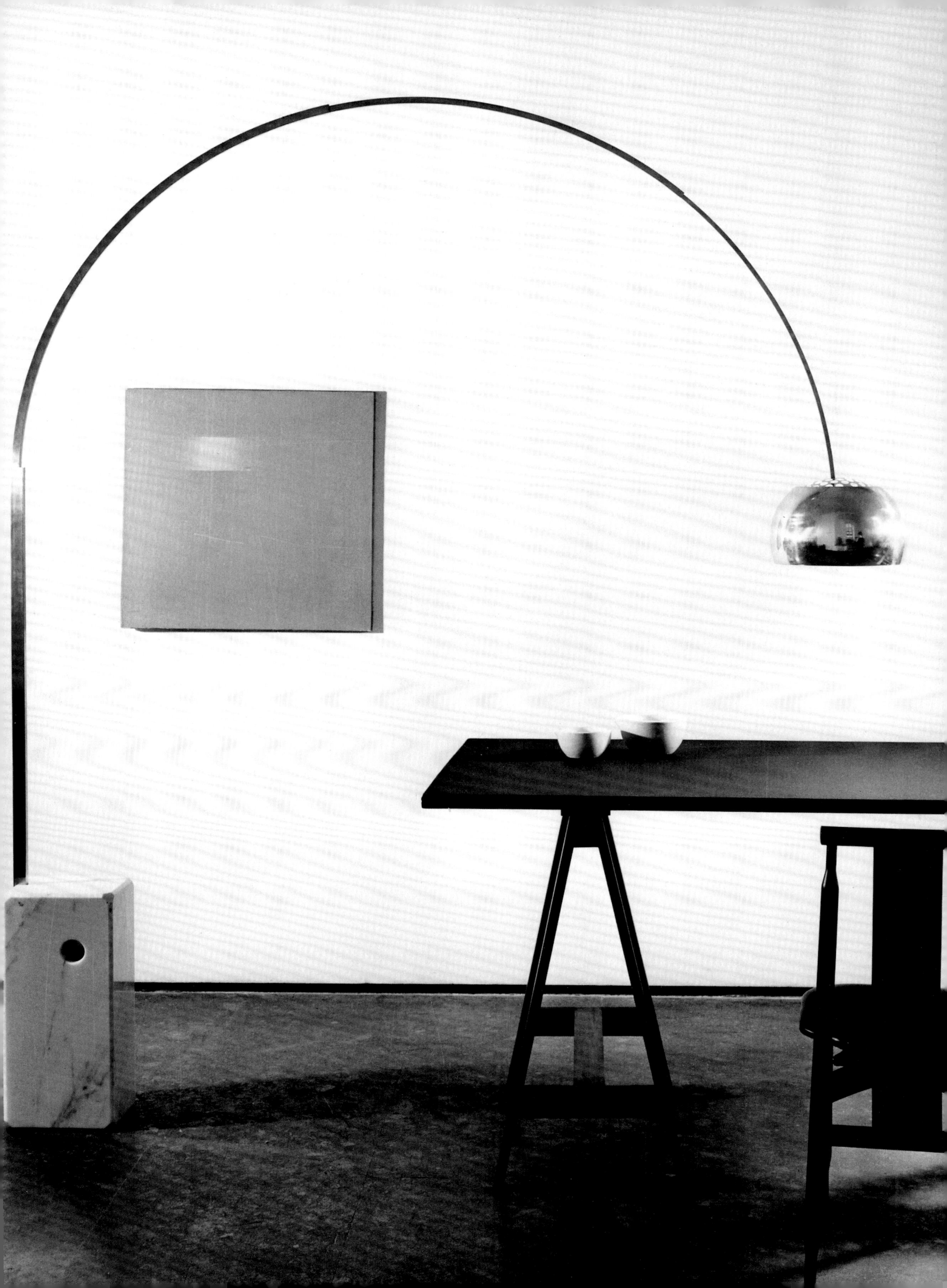

TACCIA

Designers: Achille and Pier Giacomo Castiglioni

Year: 1962

Company: Flos

Materials: table lamp providing indirect lighting, perforated chromed metal base with an anti-heat enamel coating, swivelling paraboloid in clear glass with a convex reflecting cover in white enamelled aluminium

Designed in 1958, this lamp was presented the following year in the form of a prototype at the Illinois Institute of Design and the Chicago Institute of Technology. The Taccia lamp entered into production for Flos in 1962, following its finalization. Based on innovative light-engineering (the idea of indirect lighting from a table lamp), it is a sort of sculptural icon which stands out in the domestic landscape. "It's considered the Mercedes of lamps, a symbol of success—possibly because its base is shaped like a column. But we didn't make it that way with the idea of prestige in mind, but in order to create a cooling surface" (Achille Castiglioni). The over-heating of materials was one of the main problems that had to be solved: the bulb is concealed within a chromed cylinder marked by a series of holes for ventilation; around it is a second metal "skin" varnished with black paint and moulded in such a way as to resemble the flute of a column, although it is actually modelled after car engines. This prevents light from filtering out of the side holes, while at the same time protecting one's hand from the hot cylinder. The base of the lamp may be seen as a self-standing object: an elegant cylindrical plinth enclosing a source of light. The reflector, a magical clear glass bell that looks like an upside-down ceiling lamp, is supported—without the use of any mechanical device—by the top of the base and is enclosed by a white convex aluminium disk resting on its summit. This plastic and sculptural "screen" for reflecting the light may freely be rotated on its point of support, so as to direct the reflected light in the desired direction, thus constantly changing the shape of the lamp.

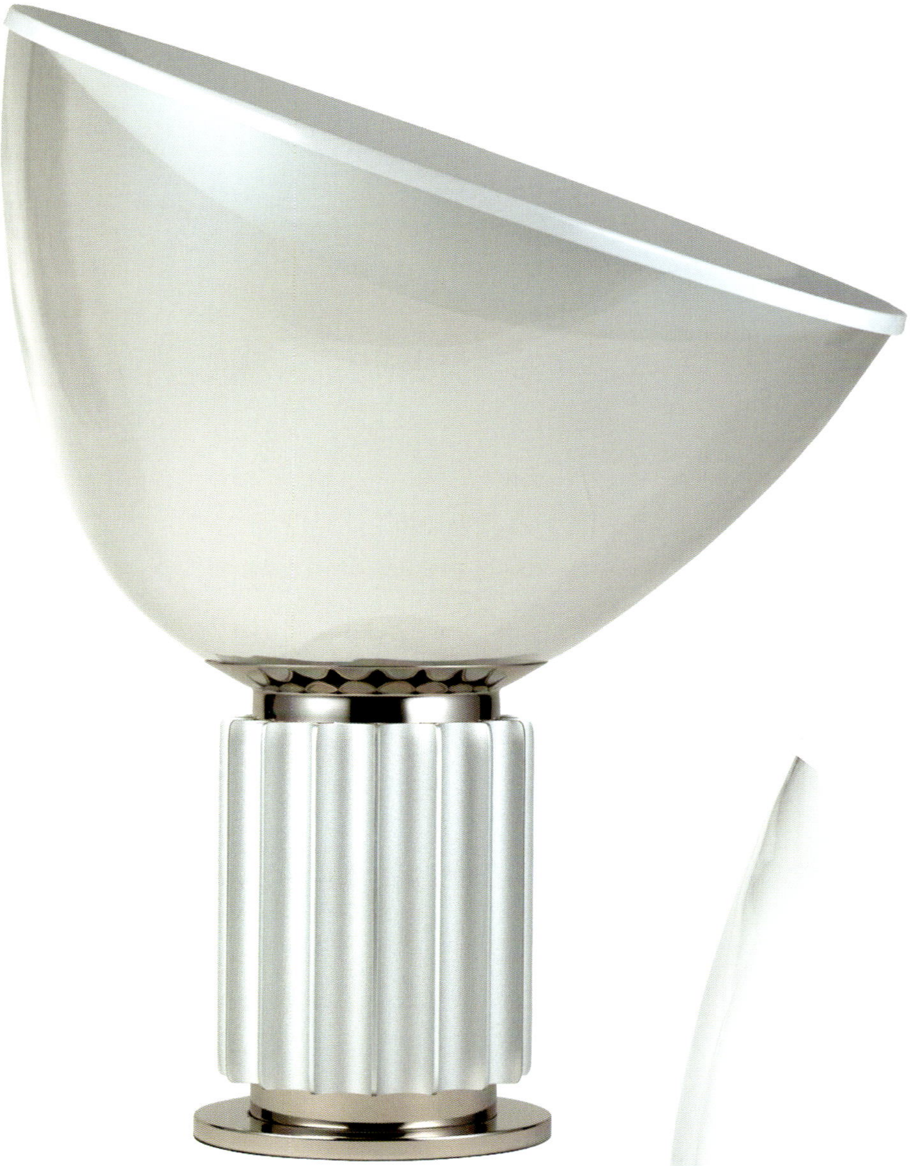

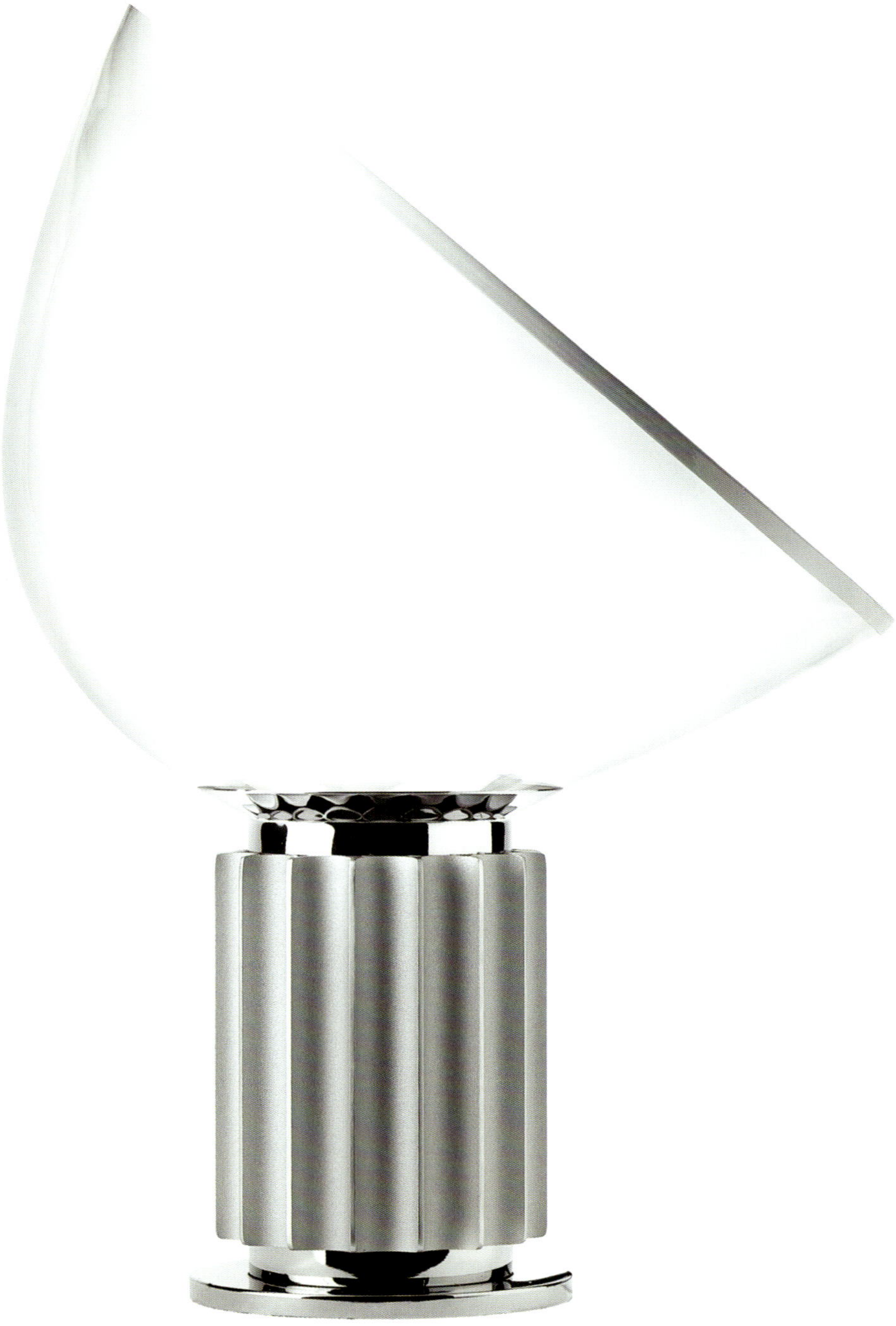

"TACCIA"
1962

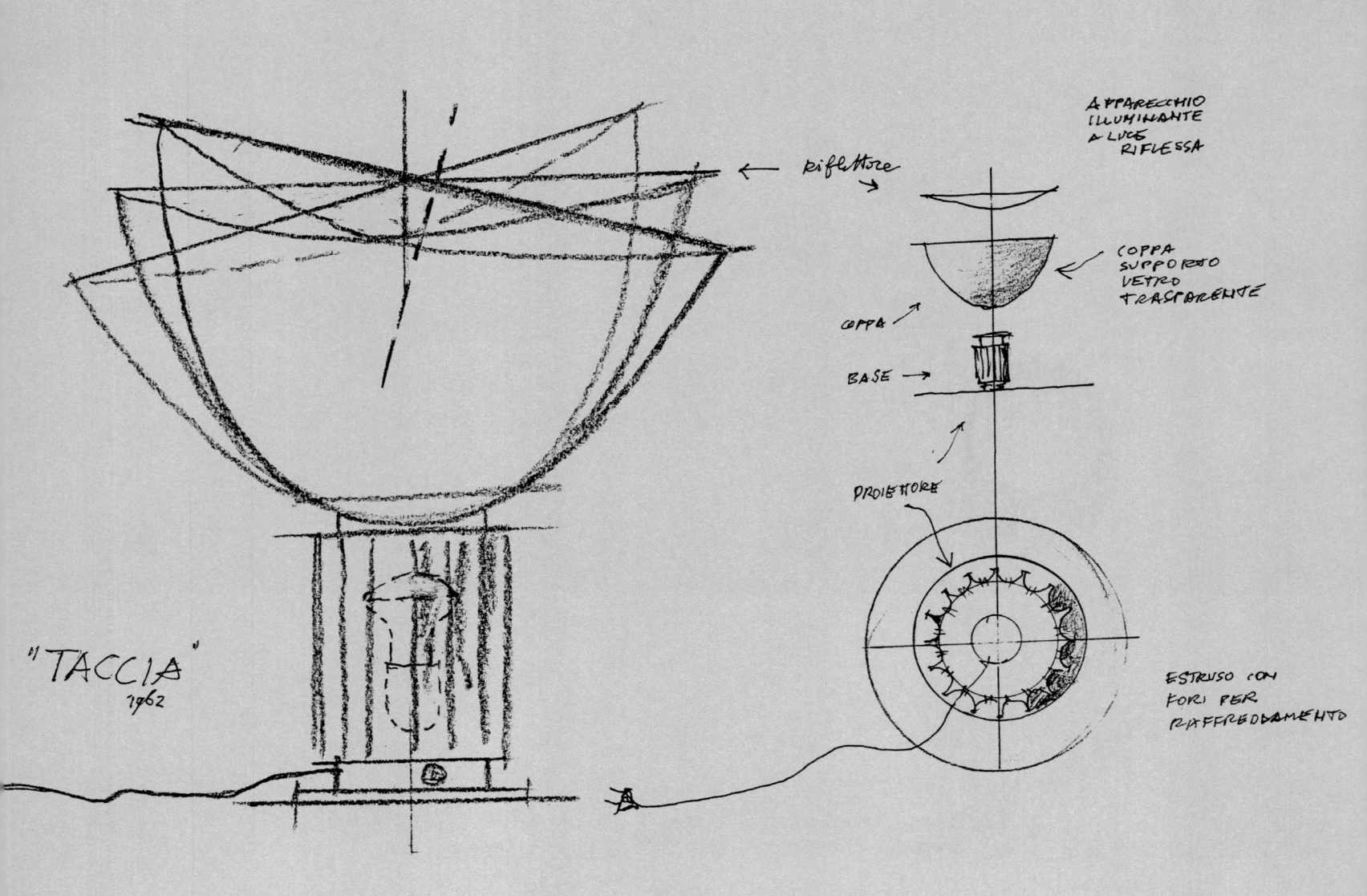

riflettore

APPARECCHIO
ILLUMINANTE
A LUCE
RIFLESSA

COPPA
SUPPORTO
VETRO
TRASPARENTE

COPPA

BASE

PROIETTORE

ESTRUSO CON
FORI PER
RAFFREDDAMENTO

91

MAYONNAISE SPOON

Designers: Achille and Pier Giacomo Castiglioni
Year: 1962
Companies: Kraft, Alessi (1996 with the name Sleek)
Material: methyl methacrylate spoon

Initially conceived as a promotional object for Kraft mayonnaise, right from the start this plastic spoon designed by the Castiglioni brothers has been not so much a "disposable" gadget as a "useful object" to be kept and stored in the kitchen drawer. "The shape of the spoon perfectly matches the inside of the mayonnaise jar, so that it can be used to wipe the neck and bottom of the container clean as well. While its handle is flat, a lunette in relief gives the thumb a firm grip on a usually slippery object" (Achille Castiglioni).
The shape of the item thus derives from the negative of the object where it was intended to be inserted. This enables the spoon to adhere perfectly to the jar for which it was conceived and hence to collect the mayonnaise without wasting any. The tip of the spoon has the same radius of curvature as the bottom side of the jar, while its straight section evenly adheres to the cylindrical wall of the jar. Finally, the top part of the spoon reflects and reproduces the profile of the section between the cylinder of the jar and its neck, enabling users to collect the mayonnaise from all areas. First created in 1962, it is now being manufactured in various colours by Alessi, which proves the endurance of the object's design and of the method behind it.

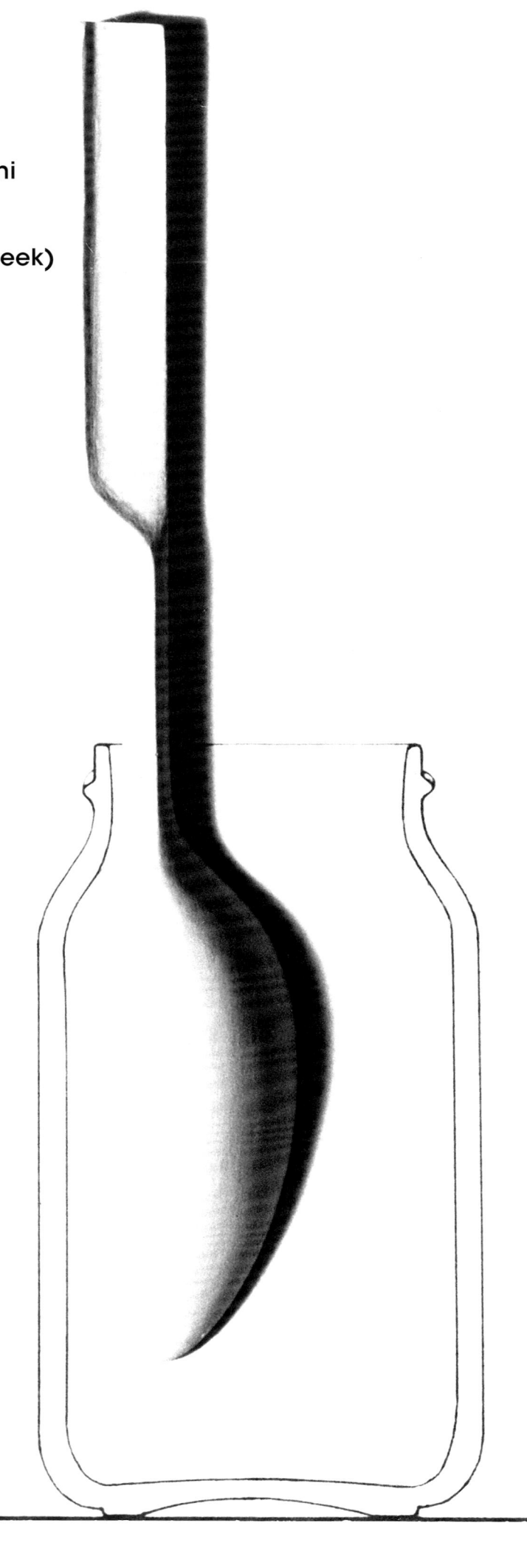

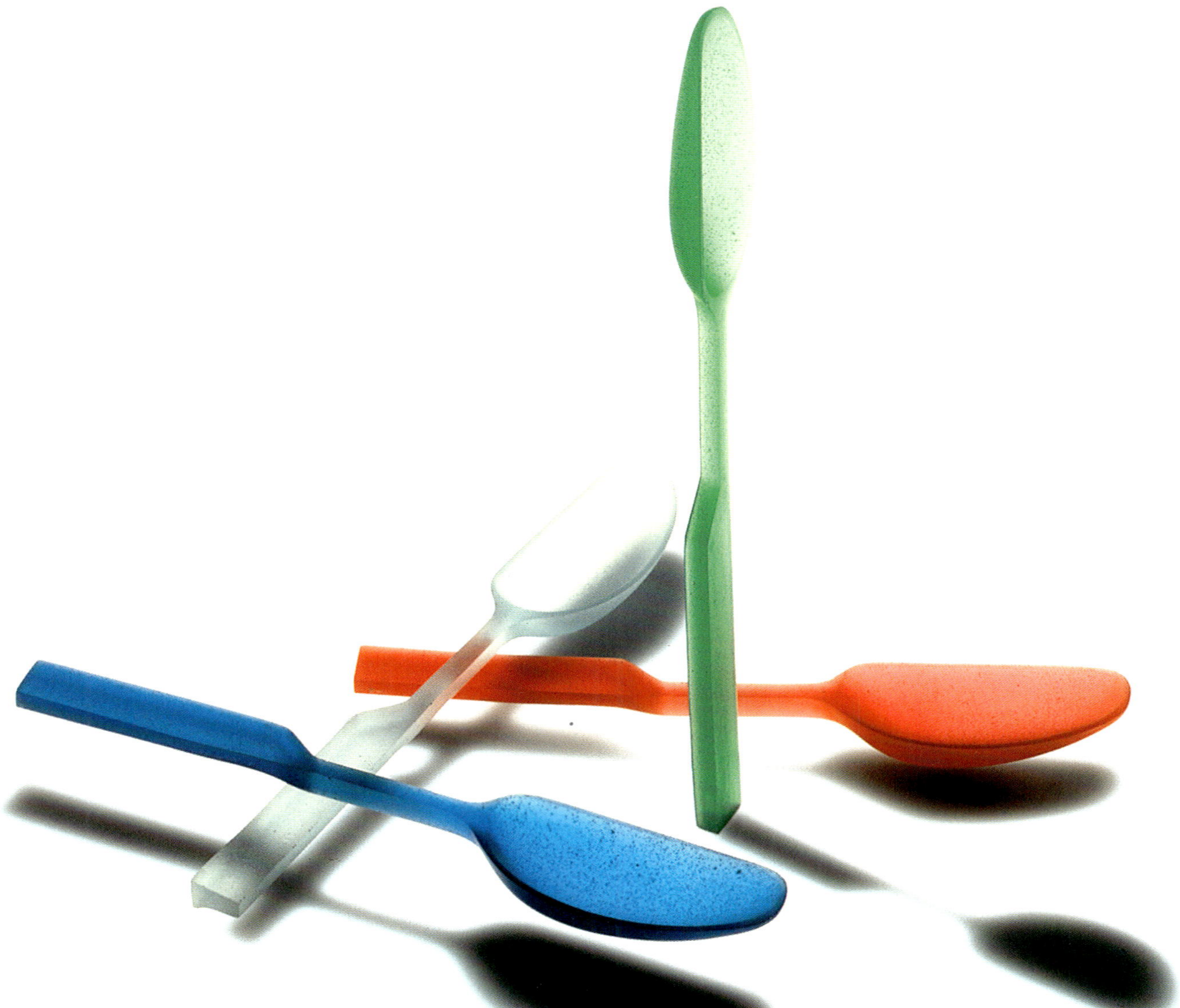

RAMPA

Designers: Achille and Pier Giacomo Castiglioni

Year: 1965

Company: Bernini

Materials: wooden structure with shelves covered by tempered glass sheets

Modelled after florists' display stands, the Rampa cabinet on wheels springs from the Castiglioni brothers' study of everyday objects as an inexhaustible source of inspiration for redesign and semantic transposition. The object also illustrates the idea of a movable piece of furniture capable of "engendering" flexible spaces—something promoted in those years by Joe Colombo. Rampa, a piece of furniture mounted on white nylon wheels, simultaneously serves as a bookcase (through its large shelves with clear glass tops), a container (through the opening front of its first component), and as a desk (through its drop-front back surface, equipped with small shelves). Thanks to its multi-functional programme, it brings freedom to domestic spaces, no longer subjecting them to rigid hierarchies based on functional arrangements. Easy to move into any room and made of pear wood, chestnut or jacaranda, Rampa enables users to create a work corner to suit their needs of the moment.

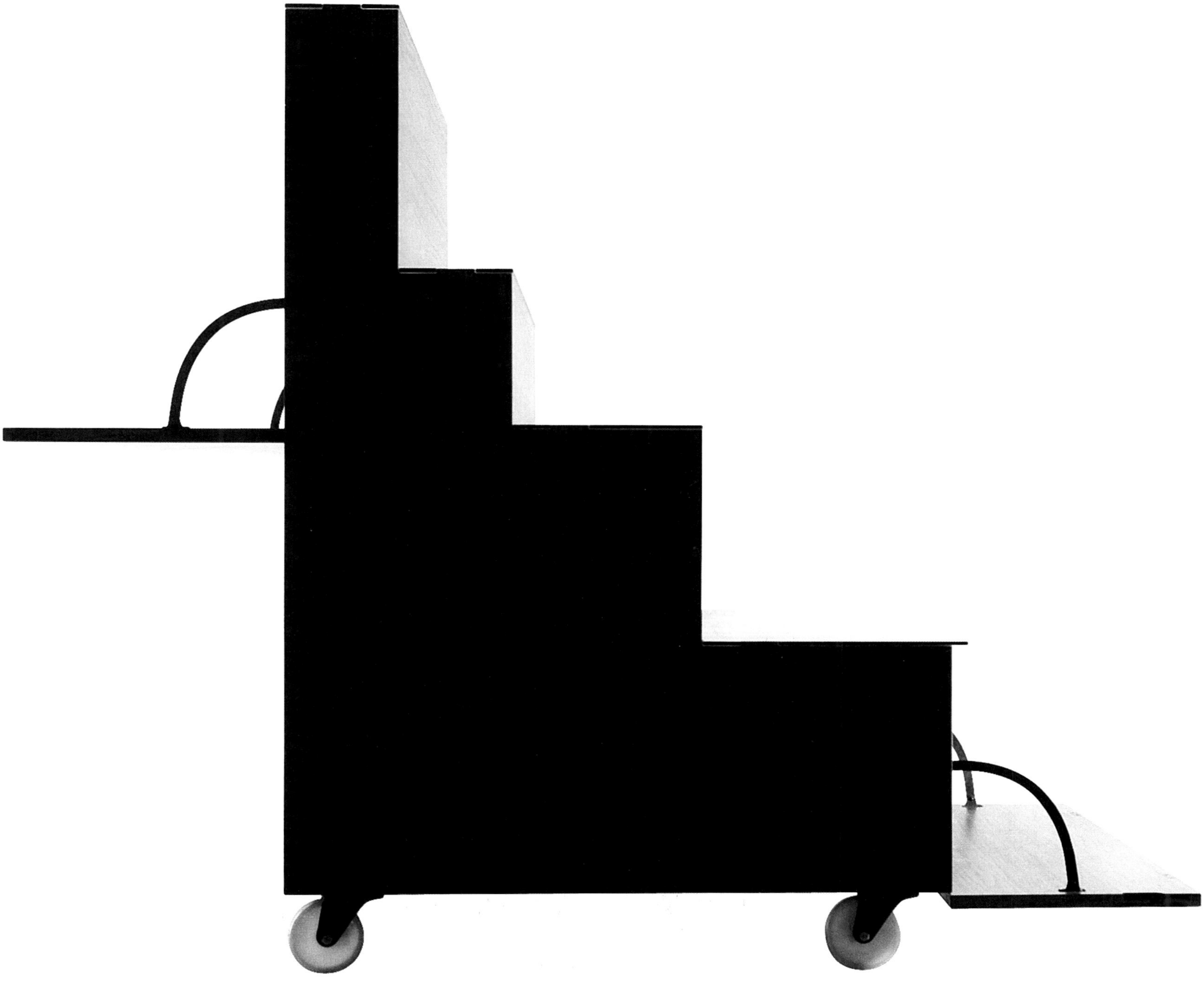

RR126

Designers: Achille and Pier Giacomo Castiglioni

Year: 1965

Company: Brionvega, BV Brionvega (2008)

Materials: lacquered wood casings, base in anodized aluminium casting mounted on wheels

The Brionvega radio-phonograph anticipated one of the aspects of contemporary design by forty years: the idea of transforming high-tech objects into "friendly" ones, in terms of both user interface and of their figurative presence in the domestic landscape. From the point of view of form, the device shows certain zoomorphic traits: metal eyebrows and eyes give it the appearance of a charming "music robot". In terms of technological performances, the object operates stereophonically (an innovative feature for semi-professional products from that period). It simultaneously functions as a record player, radio and amplifier, and may be regulated through circular displays—as opposed to the more common horizontal ones—reminiscent of 1930s radios. Finally, from the point of view of typology, the object can not only be moved on wheels, but its "free breakdown" enables three different configurations: with the speakers superimposed on the radio-amplifier-record player; with the speakers arranged on the sides, if one wishes to use the record player concealed on top of the radio; and with the speakers removed from the device and set at the corners of the room, so as to maximize the stereophonic effect.

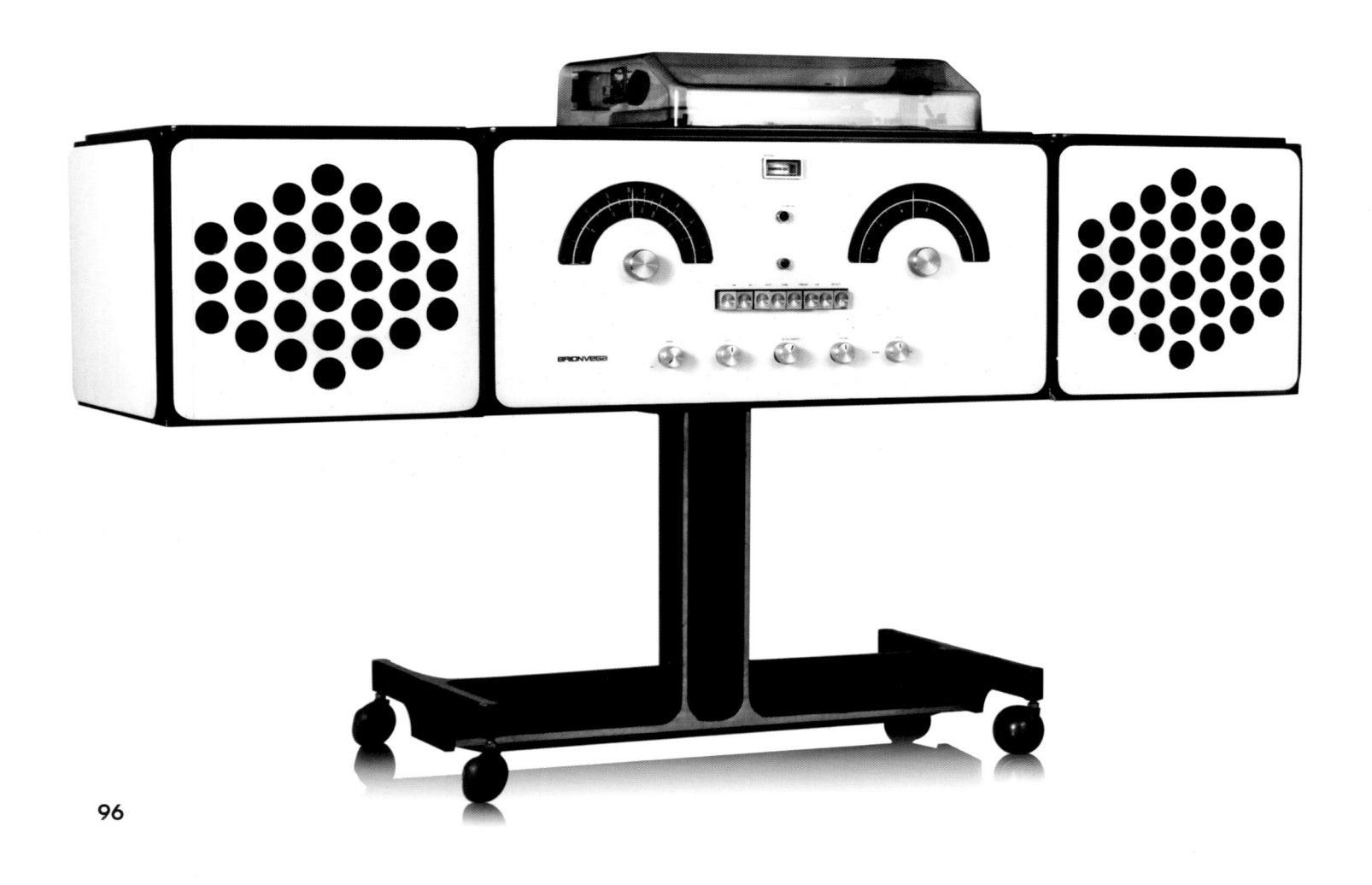

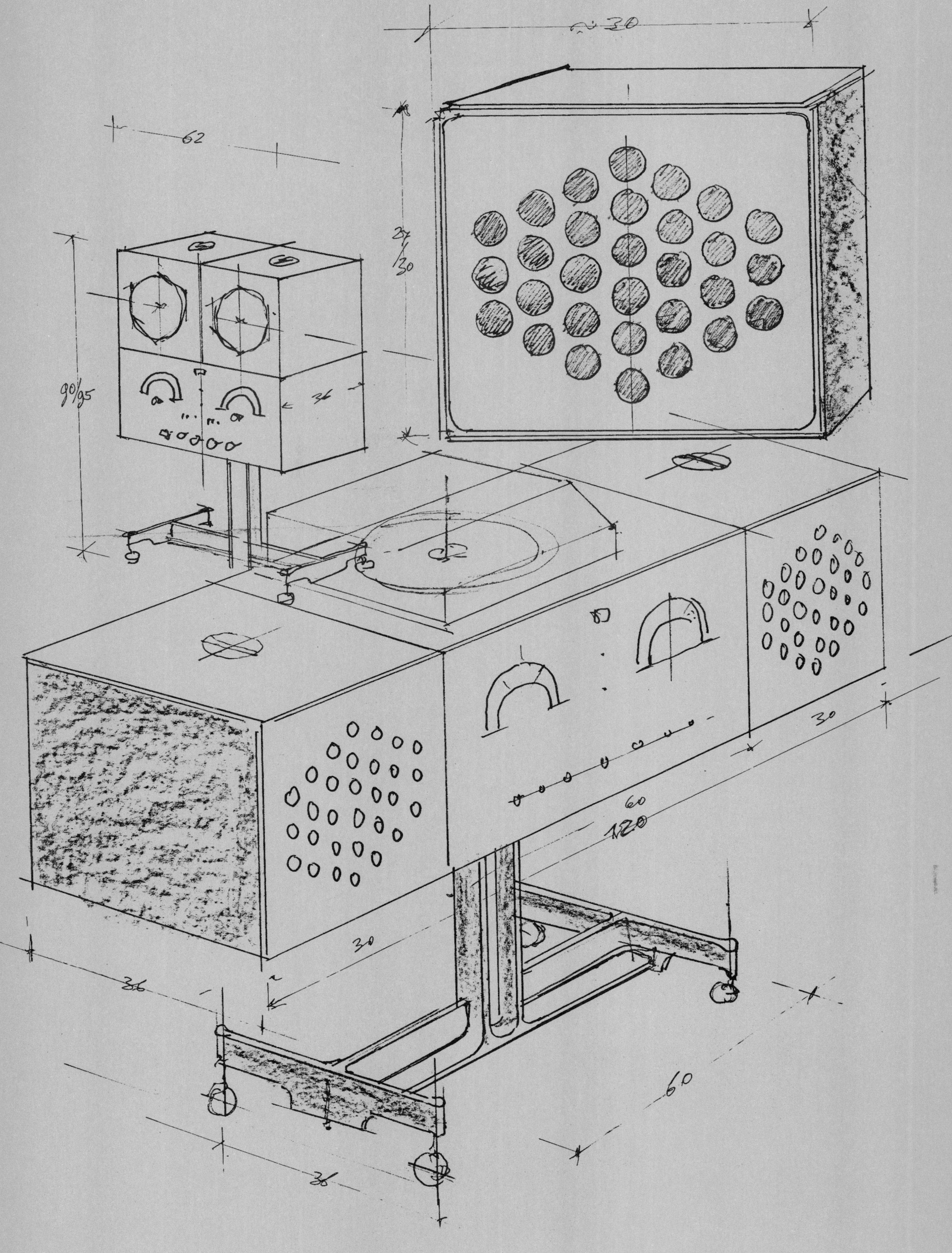

30
62
27/30
90/95
36
30
60
120
30
36
60
36

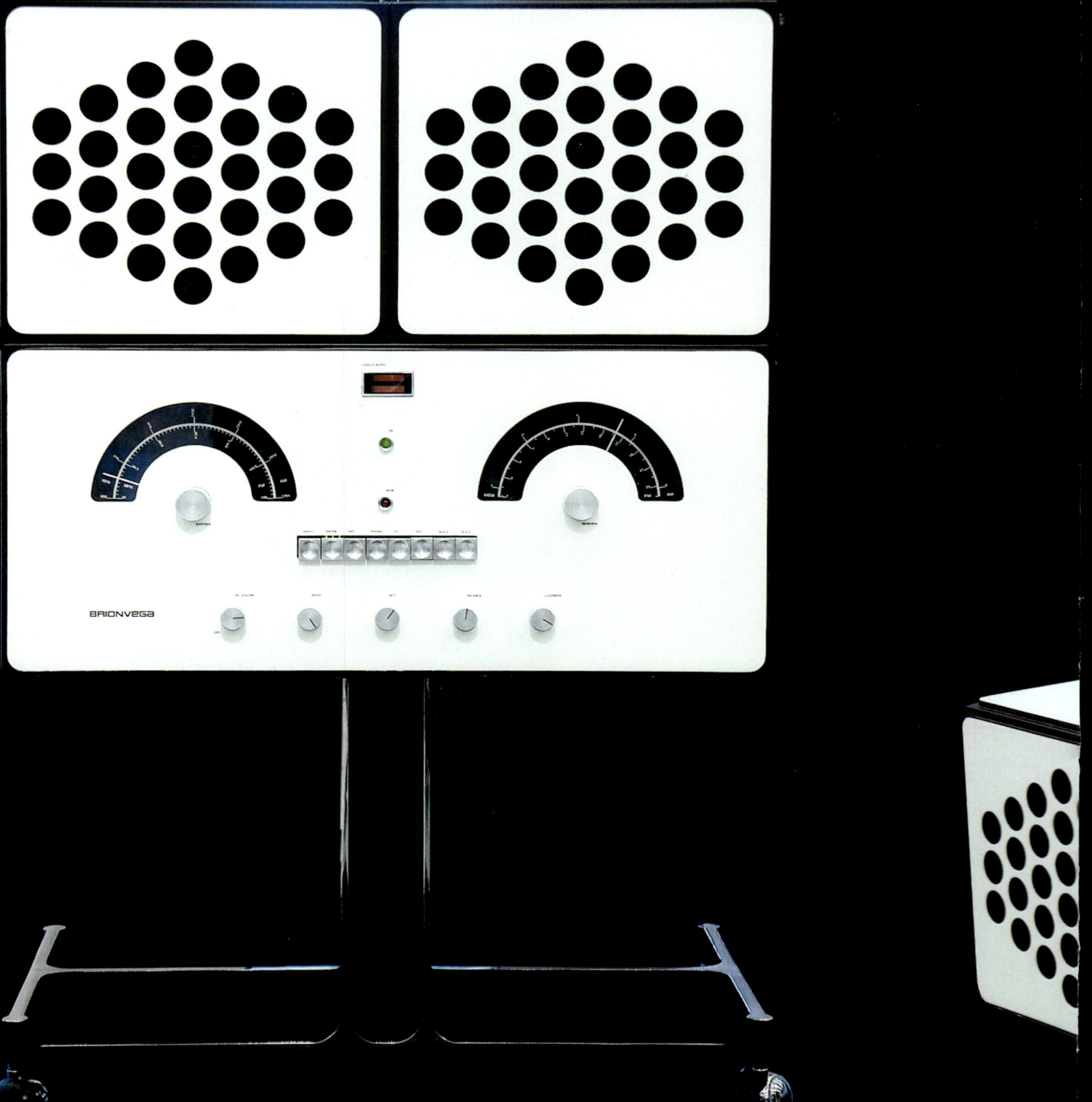
BRIONVEGA

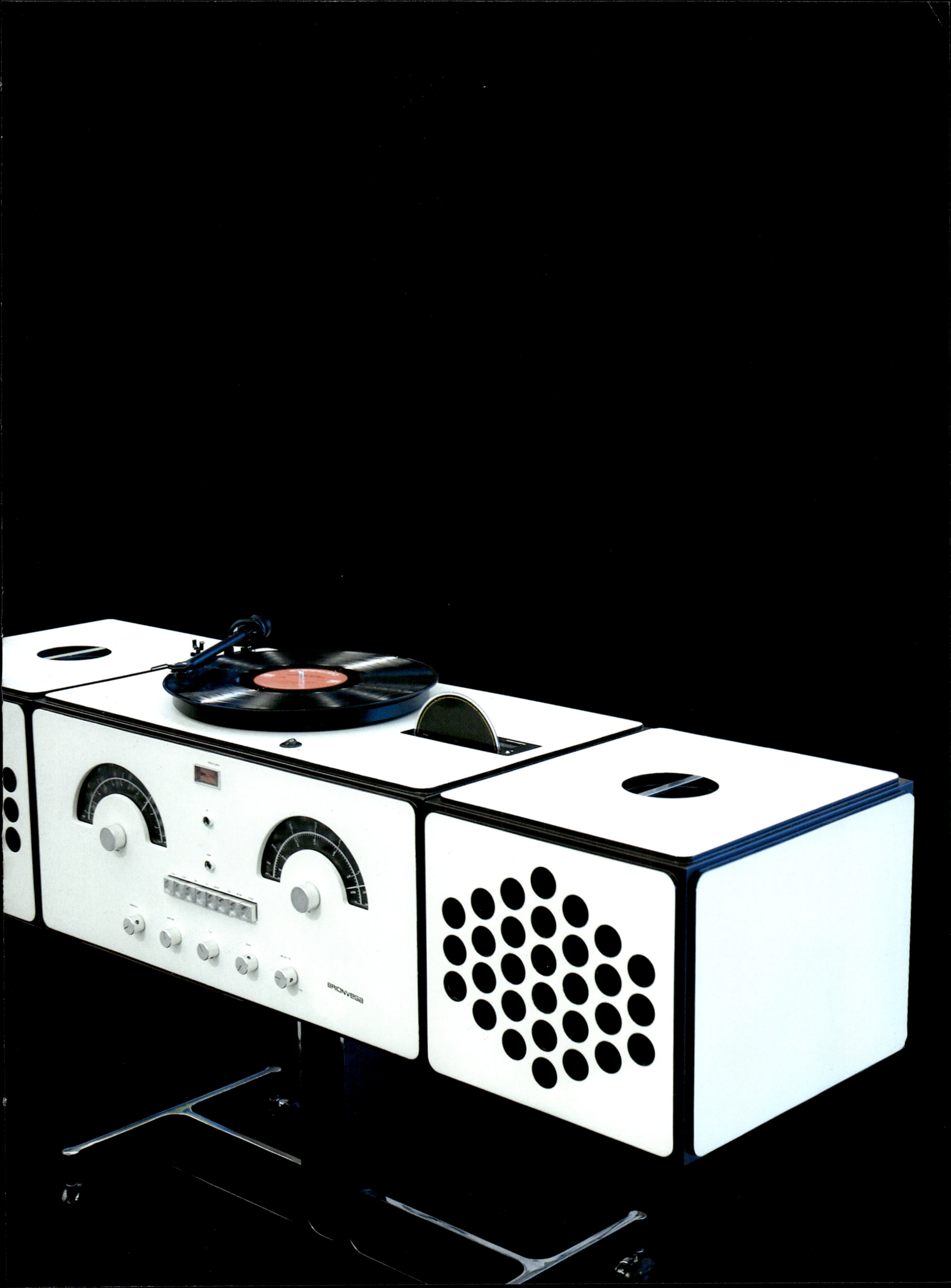
BRIONVEGA

'LA CASA ABITATA' EXHIBITION

Designers: Achille and Pier Giacomo Castiglioni
Year: 1965

The 1965 exhibition 'La casa abitata' ('The Inhabited House', curated by G. Michelucci and P.G. Spadolini, among others) was held in Palazzo Strozzi in Florence. For the first time, it provided a structured configuration of "inhabited" environments, furnished with contemporary designer pieces. The Castiglioni brothers, Magistretti, Sottsass, Ricci, Gregotti and Stoppino all sought to define a possible "system for home living" alternative to the one based on "period furniture", which dominated the market. Some of the design suggestions verged on a synthesis between interior architecture and furnishings, which were merged to provide a single plastic and compositional solution. Aside from these aspects, others emerged connected to the "way" of inhabiting a house: "this exhibition was intended to bring out those characteristics that an average inhabited house takes on when unexpected elements—necessary ones or which the family members like—are superimposed upon a pre-established order, thus engendering discontinuity and contradictions, if only apparently. (from the report issued by the Organizing Committee). Drawing upon to the message they had launched in Villa Olmo in 1957, in their proposal for a living room the Castiglioni brothers newly stressed the need to engage with "emotional objects" (a clock, a fragment from a piling attached to a wall), with anonymous design (an aluminium ladder hung like a painting, a shelf supported by black metal brackets), and with "historic" spaces, as exemplified by traditional double-wing doors in lacquered wood. These "pre-existing environmental features" were then combined with the style of contemporary design, as embodied by some furnishings and lamps by the Castiglioni brothers themselves.

TENSILE STRUCTURE FOR A RAI TRAVELLING EXHIBITION

Designers: Achille and Pier Giacomo Castiglioni

Years: 1967-1968 (Milan, Naples, Genoa, Bari)

Electronic and acoustic planning: Livio Castiglioni

A sort of flying saucer made from a translucent material, partly inflatable and capable —once fully lit—of turning into a temporary architectural signal within the urban landscape: such was the travelling pavilion designed by Achille and Pier Giacomo Castiglioni, in collaboration with their brother Livio for the electronic and acoustic features, as well as Davide Boriani and the artist Grazia Varisco for the visual design of the interior. This group and collective project foreshadowed some of the key themes of contemporary architectural research. The aim of the pavilion was to present the new radio programmes of the RAI. The setting of the interior was therefore designed in such a way as to emphasize the merging of space and light in the space open to visitors. On the stainless steel floor were projectors, lights and speakers, while the ceiling featured 864 modular elements in opalescent acrylic resin. These served as screens for the projection of the rhythmic signals of 2763 light sources synchronized with a soundtrack expressly composed by Federico Sanguigni.

The surface of the outer shell of the pavilion rested on a radial structure consisting of galvanized steel girders. Fastened to these were the cables setting in tension the small perimeter pillars supporting the locking ring under the inflatable dome. The entire structure could be mounted by five men in sixteen hours and transported on a single lorry with a trailer.

103

SINGLE-POLE IN-LINE SWITCH

Designers: Achille and Pier Giacomo Castiglioni

Year: 1968

Company: Vlm

Materials: body formed by two shells in thermosetting plastic (white urea)

With over fifteen million pieces produced, this was Achille Castiglioni's favourite object: "the object I am most proud of? The in-line switch I designed thirty years ago with my brother Pier Giacomo. Manufactured in vast numbers, people buy it for its formal qualities and no one in shops selling electrical equipments knows who designed it. It is nice to handle, makes a nice noise… When I walk into a hotel room somewhere around the world and reach for the lamp switch, it is often our in-line one I find." The body of the switch is formed by two die-cast plastic shells. The lower shell has rounded corners to facilitate moving it along surfaces, while the upper one has pointed edges and a convex shape with a circular hollow at the centre enclosing the ratchet for activating the electrical contacts. This is possibly "the most (un)known Italian designer object because it is the one most common in the real world, that with no signatures" (Beppe Finessi).

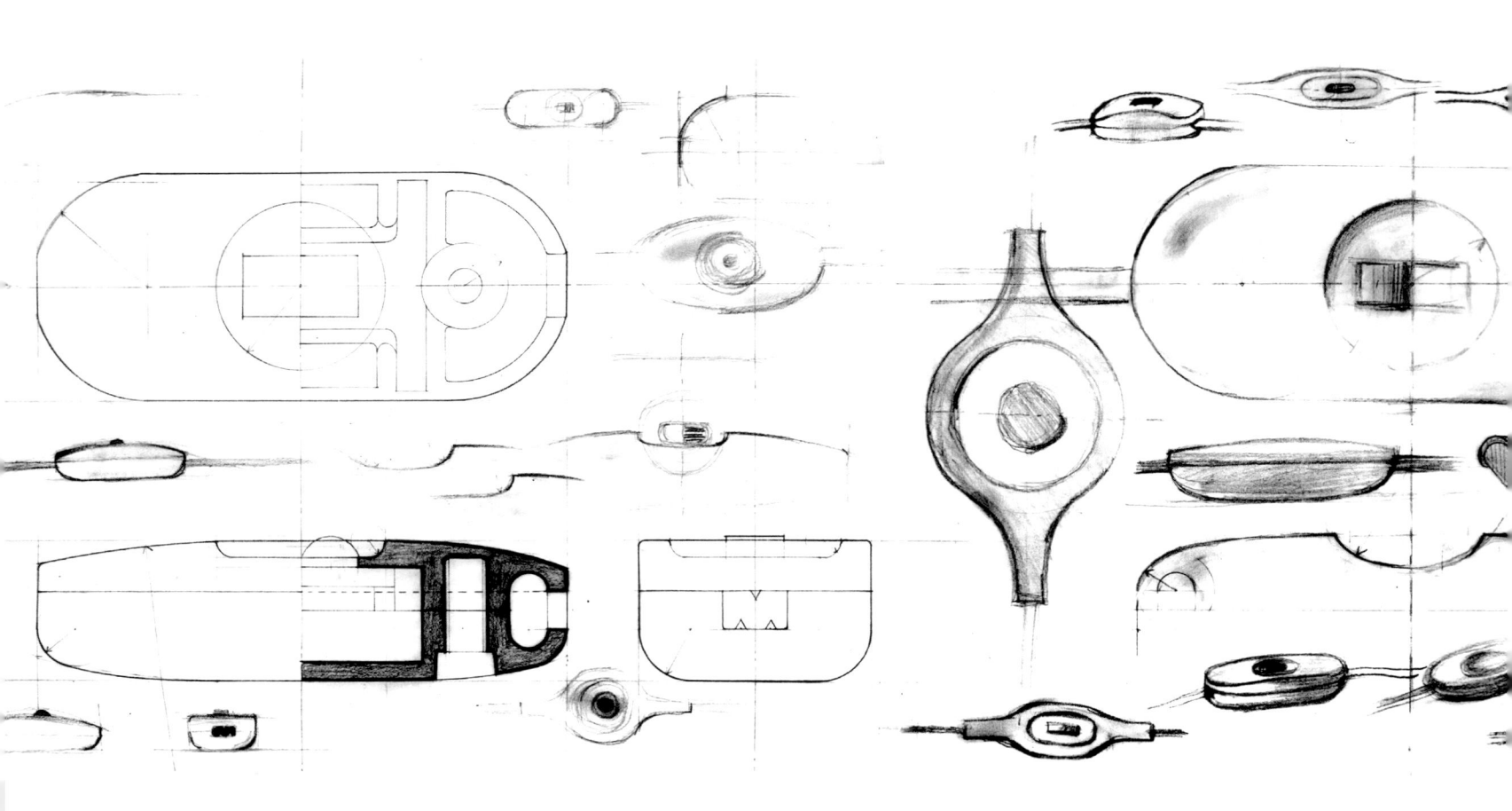

PARENTESI

Designers: Achille Castiglioni (after an idea by Pio Manzù)

Year: 1970

Company: Flos

Materials: shaped and varnished chromed tube sliding on a steel cable, rubber joint holding the socket, lead floor counterweight

Compasso d'Oro Award 1979

Pio Manzù had envisaged this as a luminous box, a fluctuating object sliding up a pole held in place by a screw between the floor and the ceiling. "I have replaced the pole with a metal cable which, when deviated, creates attrition and allows the light to remain in position without a screw" (Achille Castiglioni). Awarded the Compasso d'Oro in 1979, Parentesi newly drew upon the idea of defining the final form of an object starting from its components—in this case, a steel cable stretched between the floor and the ceiling through a cylindrical counterweight in rubber-covered lead resting on the floor, a steel boat hook attached to the base of the object, and an expansion screw with a circular enamelled disk fixed to the ceiling of the room; a socket concealed within a rotating rubber joint with a 150-watt silver-bowl spot bulb, once again in full view; and finally a bracket-shaped tube which exercises enough friction not to slide down the taut cable. Presented to the public in an especially designed kit with side handles and a vacuum-packed container in white and transparent plastic that enclosed all the components of the lamp in an almost "programmatic" manner, Parentesi ensured total flexibility in the arrangement of light within space. Intended to offer users countless ways of setting the light beam, the lamp contributes to "constructing" the space housing it without obstructing it, as it remains suspended in the air.

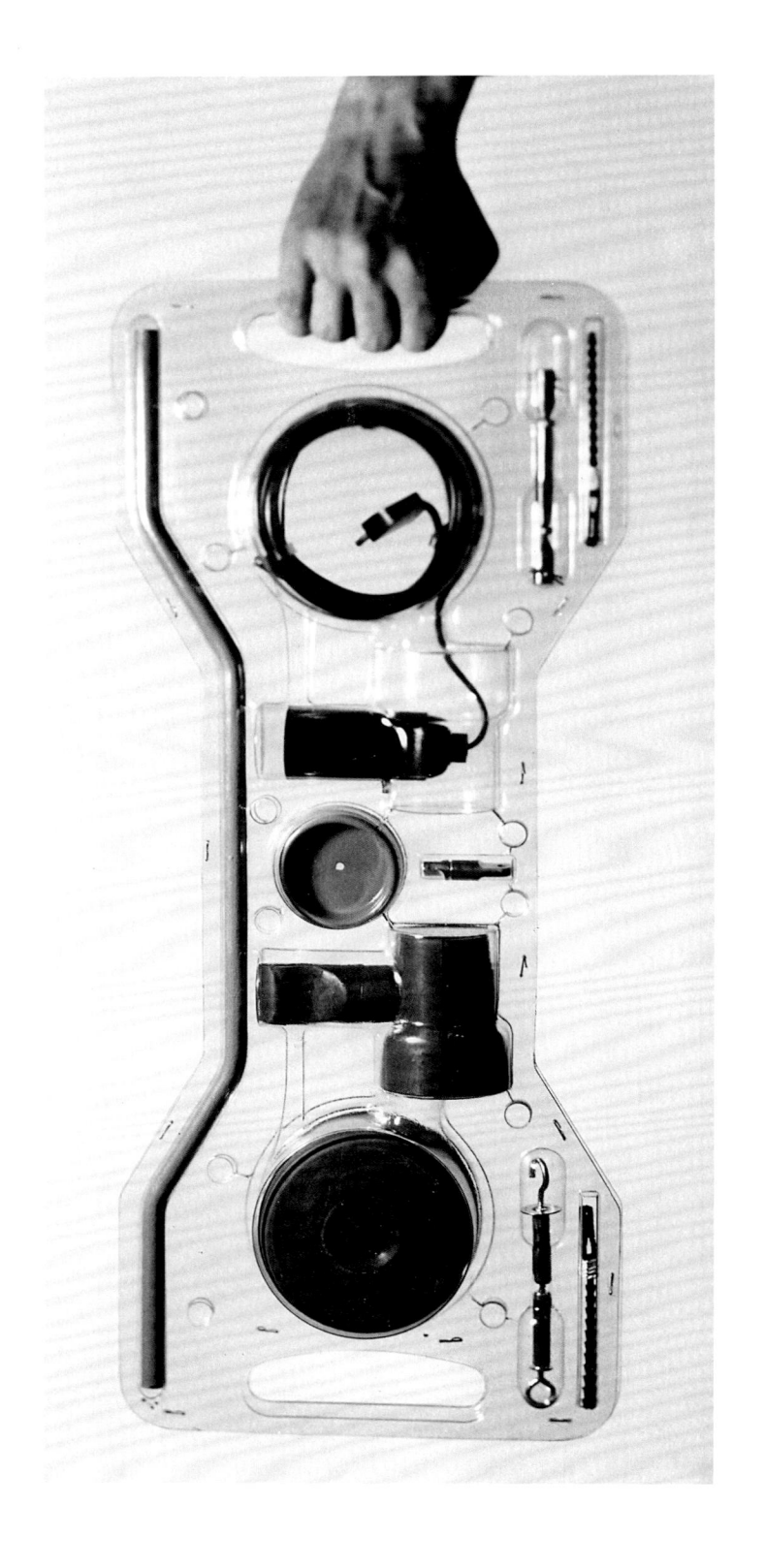

107

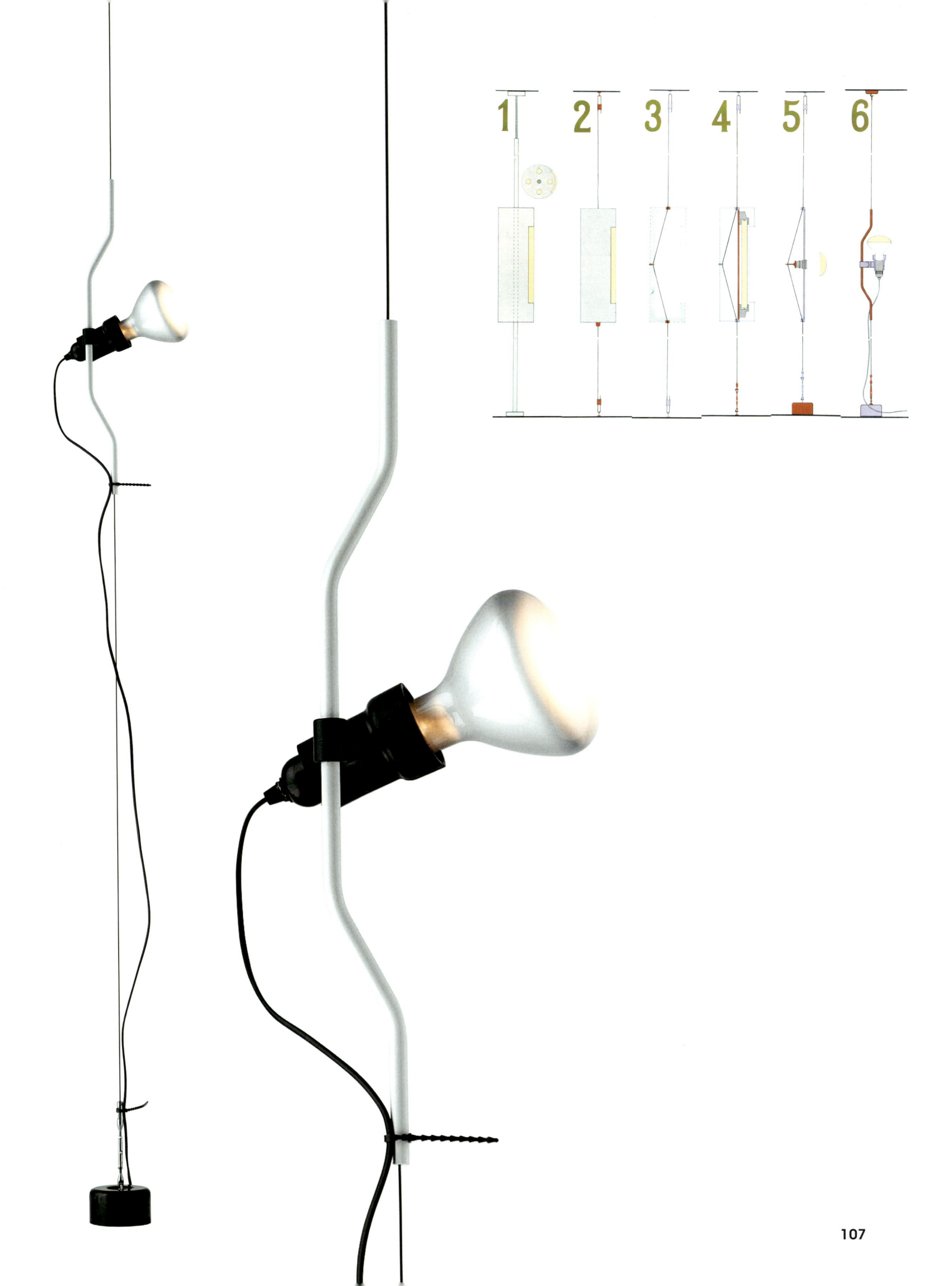

CUMANO

Designer: **Achille Castiglioni**

Year: **1977**

Company: **Zanotta**

Materials: **foldable table, stove-enamelled metal top, steel rod legs, nylon joint**

Th Cumano table, a striking example of "redesign", illustrates the underlying continuity and effectiveness of the Castiglioni brothers' method, which Achille resolutely carried on after Pier Giacomo passed away. The model of a 19th-century three-legged outdoor table with a circular top—of the sort which could still be found in Parisian bistros, as Achille observed—was broken down and carefully reinterpreted to create the Cumano. The practice of "redesign" concerns all parts of this object, which first of all was transposed from the street to the domestic environment. While the formal matrix of the original model was kept as an archetype of reference, its proportions and function were redefined. The diameter of the top was increased and the table made foldable through the addition of a nylon joint at its centre, with the straight leg passing through it, between the other two. The rod forming these legs (14 mm) was bent and flattened at its ends to create the feet of the table and the sections fixed to the rounded rim of its surface. Finally, thanks to a hole on the top equipped with a nylon hook, the table may be hung on the wall as a "discreet piece of décor" that may be put to use when required.

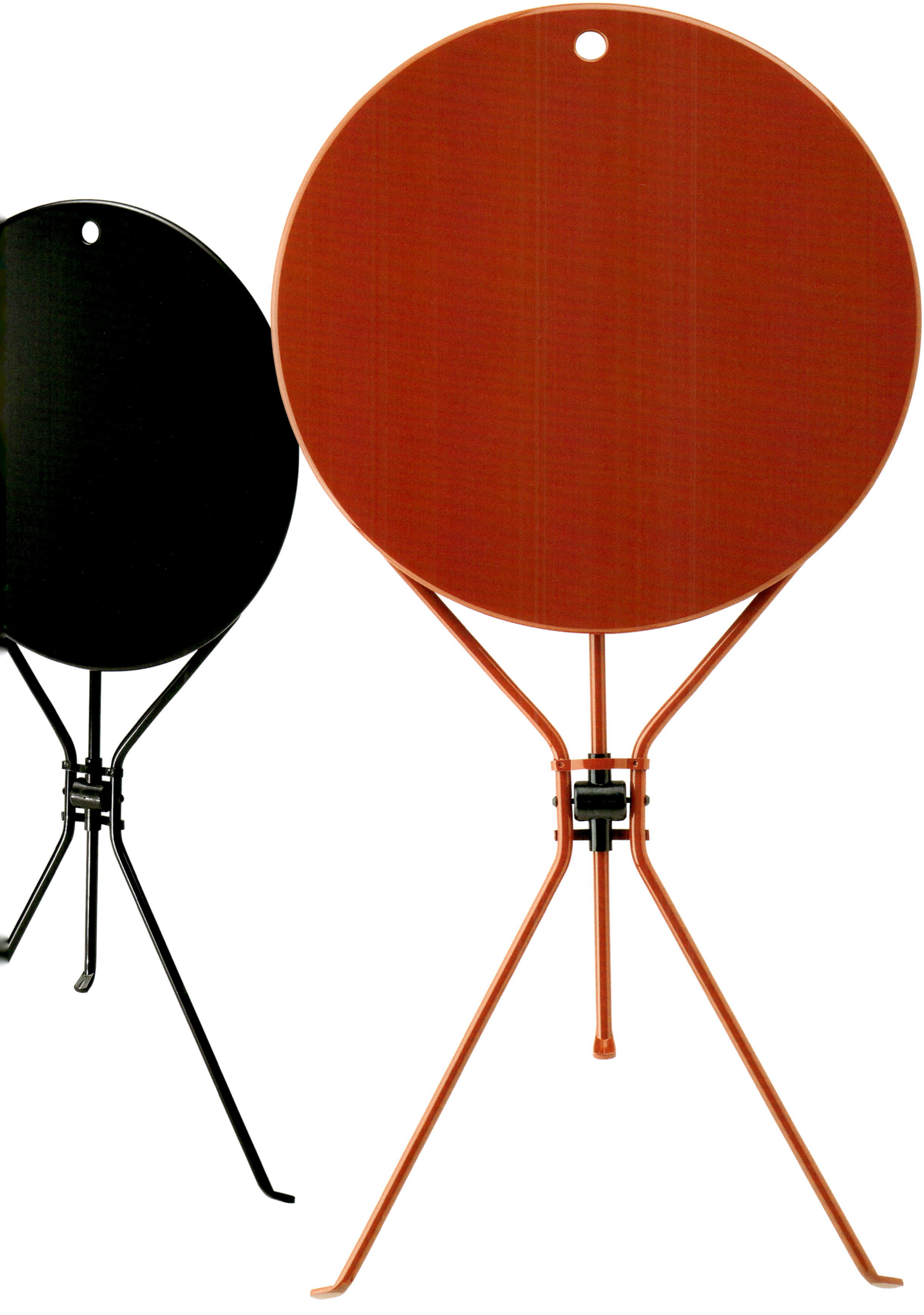

GIBIGIANA

Designer: Achille Castiglioni

Year: 1980

Company: Flos

Materials: table lamp providing directional lighting, stove-enamelled aluminium stem, halogen lighting source directed upwards, mirrored metal circular reflector equipped with a rotating plastic device

The name of this lamp comes from the Lombard term for a game that consists in reflecting the sunlight with a mirror. The idea of the project, however, stemmed from a problem connected to the use of space: some people like to read in bed until late at night, while their partners are eager to fall asleep without being disturbed by invasive lighting. Gibigiana seeks to meet this need by casting a small concentrated band of indirect light that may be regulated so as to shine only on the pages of one's book or on a given working surface, without becoming diffused. While the Castiglioni brothers had already explored the idea of a table lamp providing indirect lighting through Taccia (1962), the light in this case—which is always shone upwards—is captured by a small mirror, so as to reduce and control the glare by focusing it onto a particular spot. The enamelled aluminium stem is tapered at the front, making it easier to move it with one hand; inside it are the halogen bulb and the transformer. On the diagonally cut top of the stem is a circular reflector, fixed to a rotating plastic support of the same shape, bringing the closing circle into a vertical position.

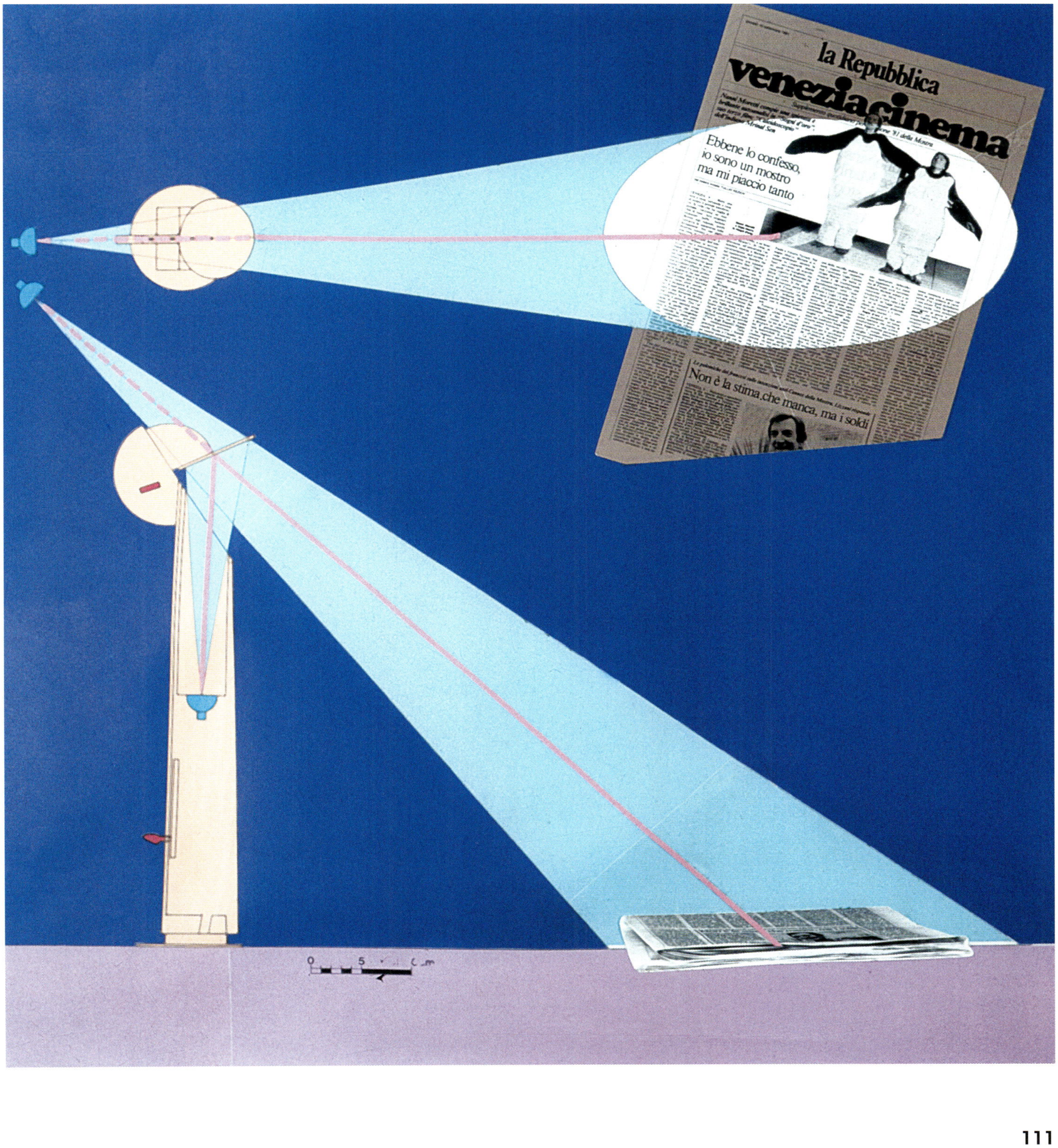
la Repubblica
veneziacinema
Ebbene lo confesso,
io sono un mostro
ma mi piaccio tanto
Non è la stima,che manca, ma i soldi

BRERA

Designer: **Achille Castiglioni**

Year: **1992**

Company: **Flos**

Materials: **diffuser comprised of two sections in white acid-etched blown glass**

This unusual example of "redesign" sets off from a historical object, a fragment in a painting by Piero della Francesca in the Pinacoteca di Brera, which gives the lamp its name. The object in question is the ostrich egg—a symbol of virginity—hanging at the centre of the *Brera Madonna* (c. 1475). It was this element, the very focus of the pictorial composition, that inspired the design of the Brera lamp, with its egg-shaped opaque white glass diffuser, which is horizontally split into two sections at the top. Fixed to the ceiling with a steel cable around which two slim and sinuous electrical leads freely flow, the lamp preserves its underlying formal unity even if it is divided in two. To the hanging version others were added—a floor, table and even wall-type—which have turned the object into a "system" by combining the egg-shaped diffuser with supporting and hooking elements in charcoal enamelled or chromed metal.

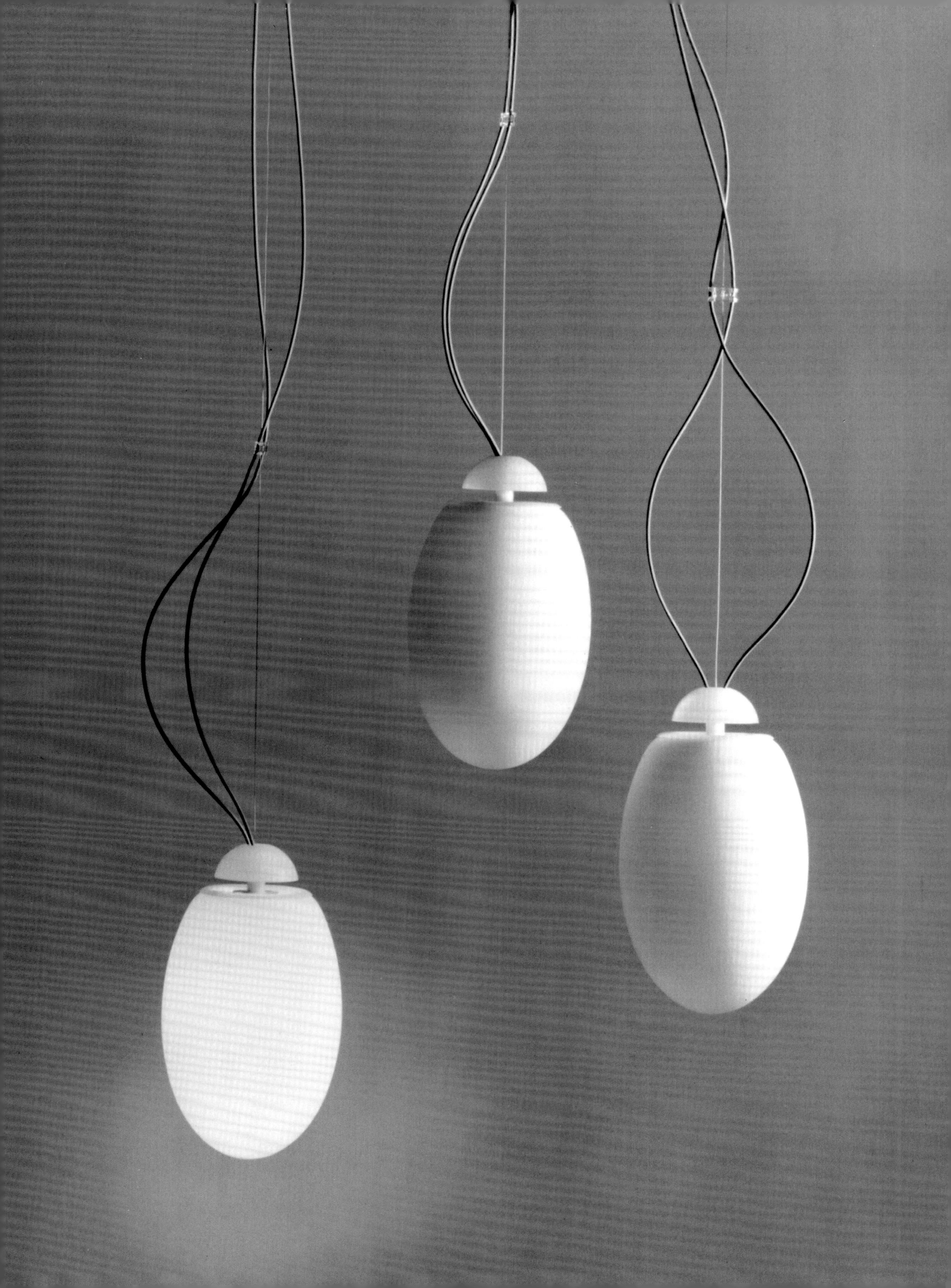

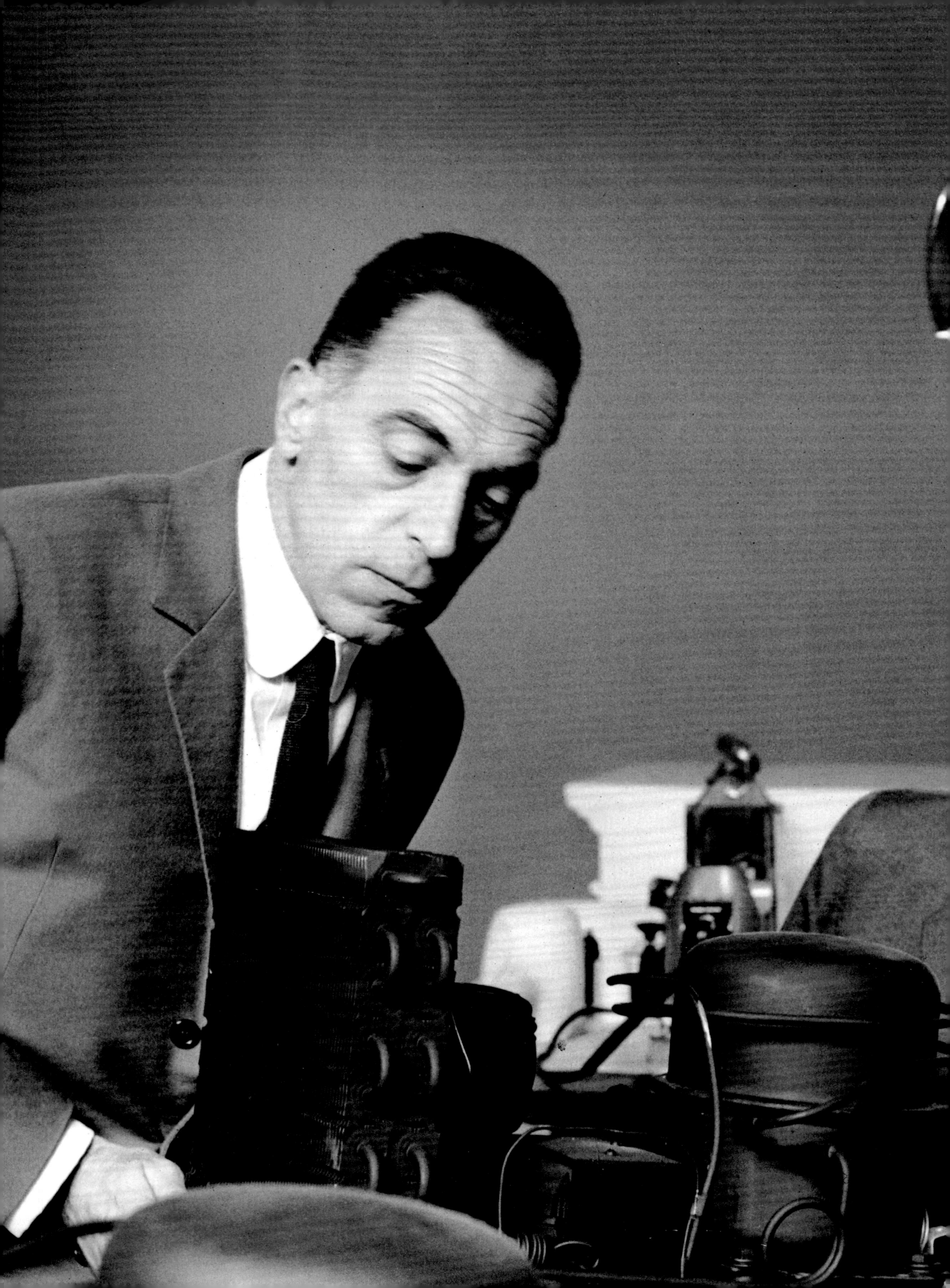

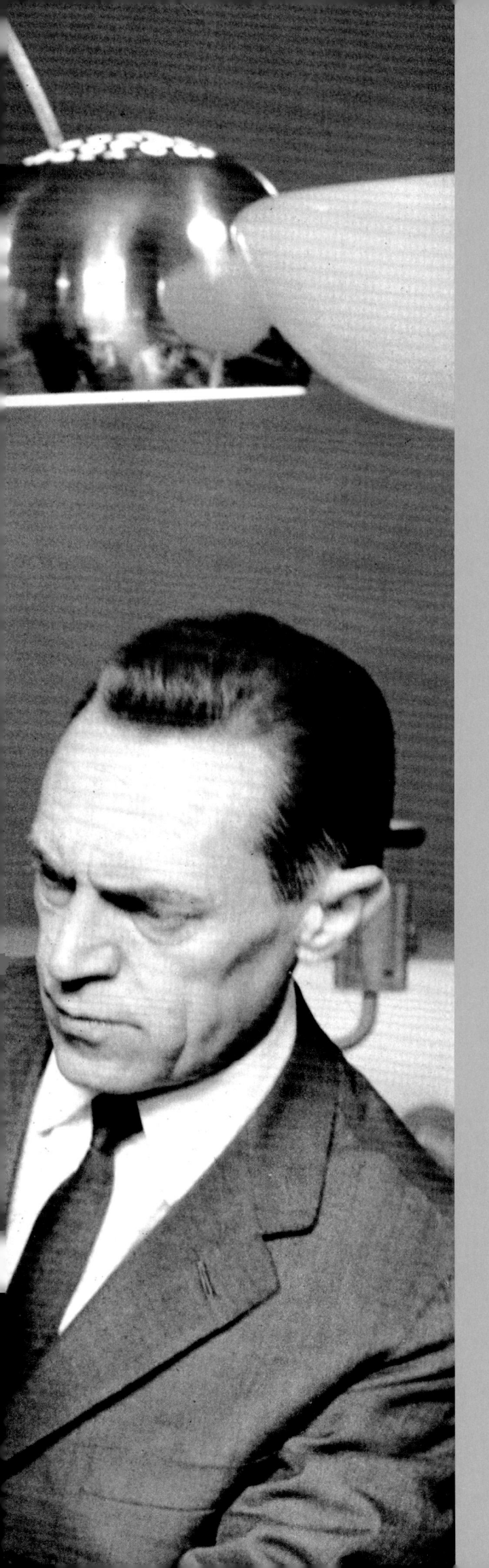

" Objects of design should not be fashionable. Fashion is made to go out of fashion, as it were. Good design must endure over time, until it is exhausted. I hate today's glamorization. My idea of designing is that of group work, not of creating projects to leave one's mark.
[…]
There is no Castiglioni style. There is a Castiglioni method. What matters is only the function of objects, their use
[…]
Experience brings neither certainty nor security. Actually, it increases the chances of error. The more time passes, the more difficult it gets to develop better designs. "

("Non c'è uno stile Castiglioni. C'è un metodo Castiglioni", in *Corriere della Sera*, 20 December 1997, p. 34)

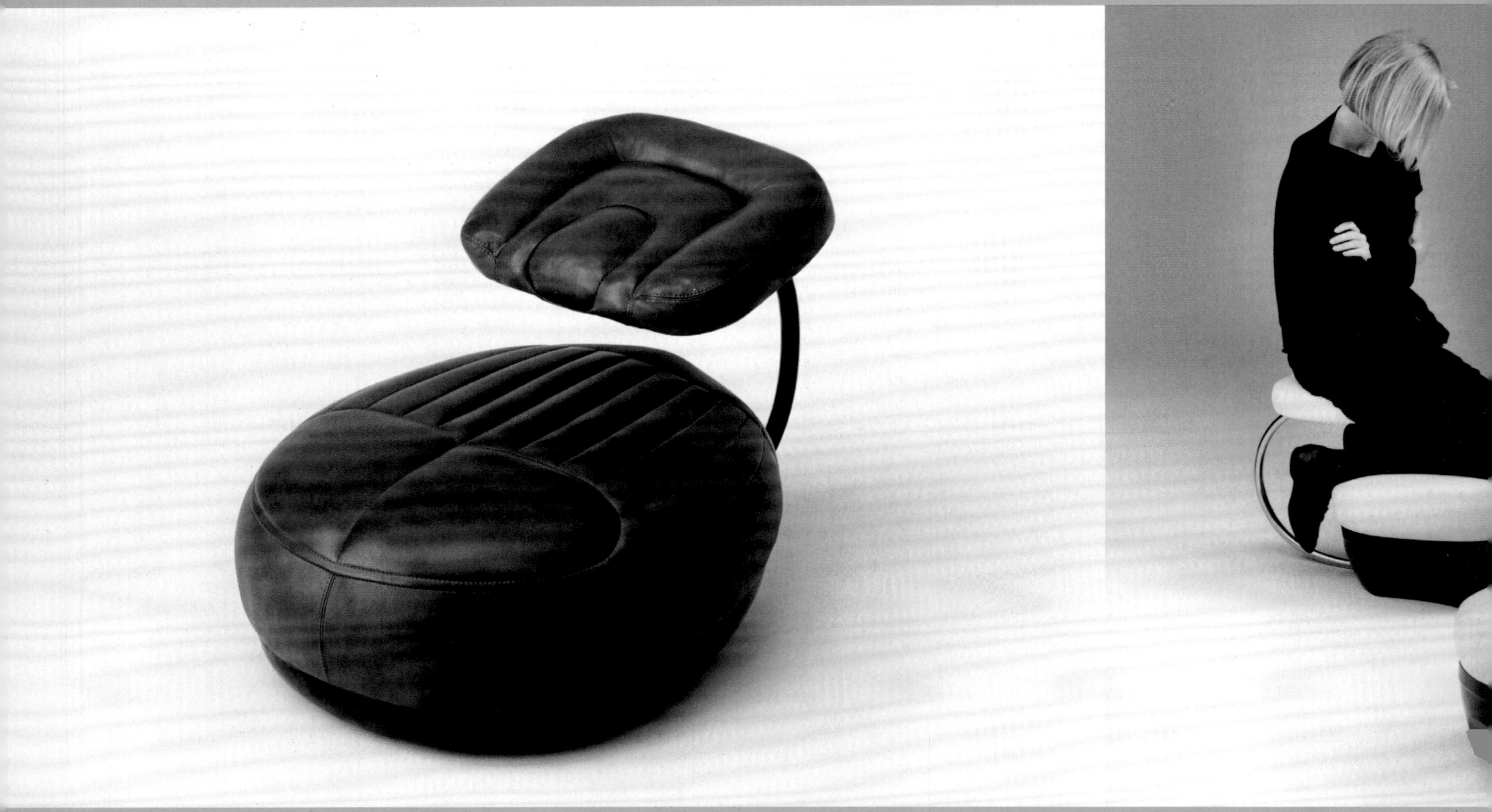

Primate, 1970

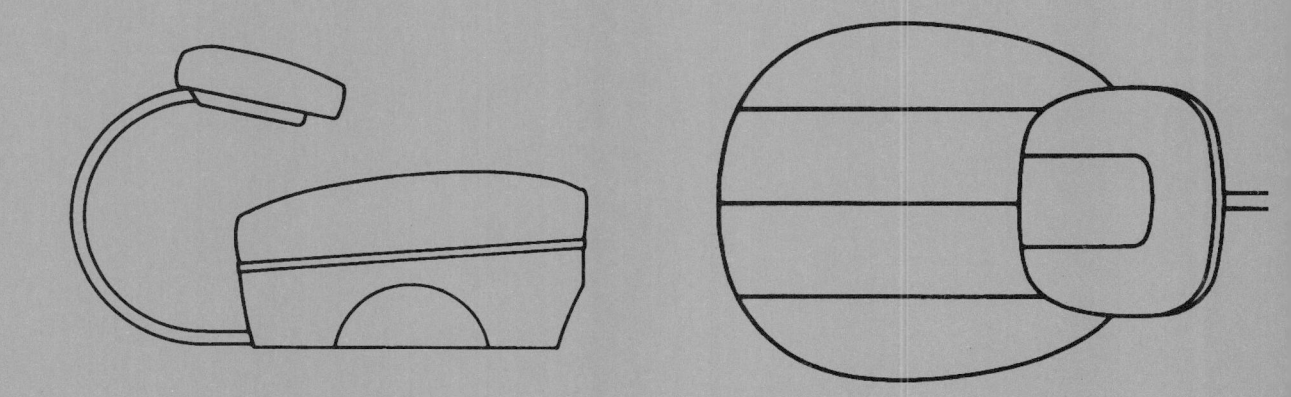

Selected References

P. Ferrari, *Achille Castiglioni*, Milan: Electa, 1984.

S. Casciani, *Mobili come architetture, il disegno della produzione Zanotta*, Milan: Arcadia Editore, 1984.

V. Vercelloni, *L'avventura del design; Gavina*, Milan: Jaca Book, 1987.

G. Bosoni and F.G. Confalonieri, *Paesaggio del design italiano 1972-1988*, Milan: Edizioni di Comunità, 1988.

Various Authors, *A la Castiglioni*, catalogue from the exhibition organized during the Spring Design Festival of Barcelona in 1995.

Achille Castiglioni, Franco Sbarro. Esperienze di architettura: generazioni a confronto, Quaderni dell'Accademia di Mendrisio, Milan: Skira, 1996.

Various Authors, *Alla Castiglioni*, exhib. cat., Milan: Cosmit, 1996.

P. Antonelli and S. Guarnaccia, *Achille Castiglioni*, Mantua: Edizioni Corraini, 2000.

P. Polato, interview with Achille Castiglioni, in *Il modello nel design la bottega di Giovanni Sacchi*, exhib. cat., Milan: Hoepli, 2000.

S. Polano, *Achille Castiglioni-tutte le opere 1938-2000*, Milan: Electa, 2001.

A. Bassi, *La luce italiana. Design delle lampade 1945-2000*, Milan: Electa, 2003.

G. Cavaglià, *Di Achille Castiglioni*, Mantua: Edizioni Corraini, 2006.

Achille Castiglioni, Museo Alessi Design Interviews, Mantua: Edizioni Museo Alessi, Maurizio Corraini, 2007.

G. Castelli, P. Antonelli and F. Picchi (eds.), interview with Achille Castiglioni in *La fabbrica del design, conversazioni con i protagonisti del design italiano*, Milan: Skira, 2007.

A. Branzi, *Introduzione al design italiano – Una modernità incompleta*, Milan: Baldini Castoldi Dalai, 2008.

A. Branzi, *Ritratti e autoritratti di design*, Fondazione Cologni dei Mestieri d'Arte series, Venice: Marsilio, 2010.

S. Casciani, *Achille Castiglioni per BTicino*, BTicino, no publication date.

Picture Credits

For all of the images © Studio Museo Achille Castiglioni,
with the following exceptions:
Courtesy of Brionvega, Pordenone: 96, 98-99
Courtesy of Flos, Merano: 10, 11, 42, 78, 84, 85, 89 above, 107 left, 110
Courtesy of Zanotta, Nova Milanese: 16, 17, 51, 54, 68 both, 70-71, 108-109
Photos by Luciano Ferri: 114-115
Photos by Walter Laeuber: 6-7
Photo by Masera: 74
Photo by Yosuke Taki: 105
IUAV University of Venice – Archivio Progetti, Fondo Giorgio Casali: 12, 62-63

Copyright holders may contact the Publisher regarding
any omissions in iconographic sources, and/or citations
whose original source could not be located.

Pier Giacomo Castiglioni (1913-1968) graduated in Architecture from the Milan Polytechnic, where he later taught Architectural Composition. In 1937, the year of his graduation, he started collaborating with his elder brother Livio. In 1944 he designed the coat of arms of the Polytechnic. Since 1952 the professional partnership between Pier Giacomo and Achille Castiglioni has brought them many acknowledgements, including a permanent exhibit of their works in the New York MoMA and five times the Compasso d'Oro award. In 1964, Pier Giacomo served as a member of the executive Technical Committee of the 13th Triennale of Milan, devoted to leisure. Together with Achille he worked in the field of architecture, the mounting of exhibits, and urban planning. He is internationally renowned for his projects connected to serial production in the fields of lighting and furnishings.

Achille Castiglioni (1918-2002) graduated in Architecture from the Polytechnic of Milan in 1944. From as early as 1940 he pursued experimental research on industrial products together with his brothers Livio and Pier Giacomo. In 1956 he was one of the founding members of the ADI (Association for Industrial Design). Achille Castiglioni's manifold interests also led him to approach the field of education: between 1969 and 1993 he taught Industrial Design, first in the Architecture Faculty of the Polytechnic of Turin and then in that of Milan. He received many acknowledgements and prizes, including nine Compasso d'Oro awards. The name Castiglioni is tied to a vast range of objects: lighting devices, radios and stereophonic devices, pieces of furniture and tableware. Achille Castiglioni was also professionally very active in the mounting of exhibitions and is remembered for the spectacular displays he created throughout the world.

Matteo Vercelloni architect, he was born in Milan —where he still lives and works—in 1961. Aside from pursuing planning work at various levels, he has collaborated with several magazines devoted to the world of architecture and design. Since 2000 he has been the editorial consultant of the magazine *Interni* and teaches the History of Design course at the Milan PoliDESIGN.